Social Intelligence Skills for Correctional Officers

Stephen J. Sampson, Ph.D.
John D. Blakeman, Ed.D.
Robert R. Carkhuff, Ph.D.

HRD Press, Inc. • Amherst • Massachusetts

Published by: HRD Press, Inc.
                  22 Amherst Road
                  Amherst, MA 01002
                  800-822-2801 (U.S. and Canada)
                  413-253-3488
                  413-253-3490 (fax)
                  www.hrdpress.com

ISBN 0-87425-858-8

Production services by Jean Miller
Cover design by Eileen Klockars
Editorial work by Sally Farnham

Table of Contents

Preface

Most training programs for correctional officers have focused on security or custody skills: conducting counts, shake-downs, riot control, and report writing. But most correctional officers would concede that they learn their "real" skills from the experienced officers encountered and by trial and error. In addition to the security responsibility, officers are required to "supervise" inmates. (We have chosen to use the terms *manage* along with *supervise* and *inmate* interchangeably with *detainee*.) The typical officer becomes a logistics specialist, keeping track of the whereabouts of all inmates in his or her assigned area and seeing that they all get to and from the activities within an institution. In addition, officers are a major source of information for detainees and are general ombudsman.

Recently, the officer's role in the inmate's rehabilitation has been a concern. Recognizing the ratio of officers to inmates and also their physical closeness, corrections administrators and officials are beginning to accelerate their concern about the officer's responsibilities in the rehabilitation area.

Investigation into the factors influencing inmates in corrections settings found that half of the released inmates studied cited a corrections staff member, especially the work supervisor, as the most influential force in their reformation.

Training programs for officers often do not include any "skills" training that focuses on influencing the relations of officers with inmates. This is in spite of the obvious importance of human relations skills. Even when training does attempt to effect positive relations of officers with inmates, it tends to be conceptually based rather than skills based. This means that the most common training method used is lecturing to officers about what they "should" think and how they "should" act. Little opportunity is provided officers to "try out" new ways of managing inmates, which might help reconstruct their attitudes and contribute to eventual rehabilitative efforts. Correctional officer attitudes about inmates most often either remain what they were (negative) or are influenced by the officers whom they encounter during their probationary period (frequently negative).

When there is some form of human management skills pre-sented in the correctional training of officers, it tends to be of short duration (seldom more than 20 hours) and often is given low priority, even though the realities of institutional supervision will place inmate and officer in daily interpersonal contact, for better or for worse.

An additional problem confronting training is the lack of follow-through to ensure that learning that is translated into officer behavior is sufficiently rewarded. Too often, the trainee hears the statement from the experienced old hand, "Now you can forget all that philosophizing they do at the training academy and learn from me how to handle these convicts." It is obvious that those who wish the officer to be skilled must pay the price to learn the skills as well. You cannot be anointed with skills; they must be learned.

IPC: Interpersonal Communication Skills for Correctional Management is based on correctional officer training programs that have been successfully implemented in federal and state correctional systems for several years. It is built on nearly two decades of research into the effectiveness of staff interpersonal skills training, and on inmate populations and other populations in need of help. The program itself is an application of these skills training programs to the staff management of correctional inmates.

The skills taught in this revised and extended manual will be the same skills taught in the earlier edition of *IPC: Interpersonal Communications Skills for Correctional Management.* These skills are based on a philosophy developed by Dr. Robert R. Carkuff. The application of his philosophy and skills to training programs has been far-reaching and enormously successful. His theories are widely used to assist in the training of professional helpers, paraprofessionals, and those who want to improve their impact on others who they encounter such as family members and co-workers.

The context of this manual is a corrections setting like the origi-nal manual. Scenarios that include the management of mentally ill detainees have been added. Inmate populations have surged as state institutions have been closed and budgets for the care of the mentally ill have plummeted. Training officers to manage mentally ill detainees has not kept pace with their increasing numbers. New medications have also made it more likely that the mentally ill will be absorbed into general populations.

IPC is the term that correctional officers used to identify the skills training that they helped shape through their contributions. Many skills training programs are now successfully taught by officers just like you. Accordingly, we gratefully acknowledge their participation and dedicate this book to them for the development of effective correctional officers and the consequent effective management of the inmate populations.

Introduction

Due to the increased awareness and knowledge about mental illness (MI) in our society, it is no surprise that we find large numbers of the mentally ill incarcerated. Mental illness is defined differently by different stakeholders. At the risk of ignoring or even offending some of them, we are not going to attempt to clear this up. If you use the definition that your institution uses (the one that your medical staff uses), it will be sufficient.

The arguments about the causes will not affect your management very much, if any. Research indicates that as many as 40 percent of persons diagnosed with MI have a heritability factor. Families with a history of MI have a propensity for some forms of MI more than others.

As far as detention populations, it appears that about 20 percent of a typical population is considered mentally ill. Each facility is different, but the medical staff who dispense medicines can give you a quick estimate of the number of detainees who are prescribed neuroleptic and other types of meds generally associated with those who have severe and persistent mental disorders. Numbers and percentages vary widely due to definitions and screening, but we are talking about large numbers.

Given the high incidence of substance abuse associated with detainees (some say 80 percent), some confusion is also encountered in sorting out symptoms and classifying the MI substance abusers and others who are dually diagnosed. Usually the behaviors and symptoms associated with substance abuse fade rather quickly as the effects of the substances are washed from the body systems, and the symptoms associated with mental illness are lessened as soon as the appropriate medications take effect. However, the symptoms of MI can still be quite visible. Your medical staff will eventually sort all this out over time. It often takes considerable time for the correct medications and dosages to achieve results.

If after the application of the generic skills introduced in this manual no improvement is noticed in your management efforts, you may guess that a detainee may not be adequately medicated or there may be some physical disease process affecting the behavior. Keep in mind that medications often cause side effects that produce symptoms themselves.

Externally you may notice twitching, skin discoloration, tongue thrusting, changes in gait, and more. Internally, there may be cramping, diarrhea, nausea, fatigue, etc. Always check with the medical staff when you observe any of these changes. Although very quiet, submissive detainees may be a joy to manage, but they are often overlooked. Check them regularly.

The materials in this book are divided into three major sections:

I.   The Basics: Sizing Up the Situation
II. The Add-Ons: Communication with Inmates
III. The Applications: Controlling Behavior

In each of these three sections, you will learn some very specific skills—skills that have already been demonstrated to work. You'll have a chance to practice the skills and see how well they work for you. You'll be able to help refine the model used to teach these skills by having input into your own training. Finally, you'll have opportunities throughout your training to put your own personal experience in correctional work to use.

Frustration, tension, violence, and a host of other "old" problems still exist in corrections. They exist because until now, correctional officers had to rely on old and ineffective solutions. Yet all this can change—and you yourself will become the agent of this constructive change as you begin to master the skills in this manual.

Section I

The Basics:
Sizing Up the Situation

Example **What's it all about?**

An inmate approaches the correctional supervisor's area. He is restless, breathing quickly, repeatedly clenching and unclenching his fingers. His eyes are wide open and his lips are twitching slightly, but the officer doesn't notice these signs. He's busy going over the morning call-out sheet. His workstation is situated so that the inmate is not in full view. The officer would have to make a 90-degree turn to see the inmate fully.

The inmate appears to want to speak to the officer. He is mumbling. Deep into his work, the officer indicates that and tells the detainee to come back later. A short time later, there is a shout from another inmate in the unit that something is wrong. He points to the recreation area that is adjacent to the unit. There lies the inmate who had earlier approached the officer. According to the detainees the detainee who was lying motionless had charged across the rec area and rammed his head into the concrete wall. He was taken to the emergency room of the local hospital and later treated for cervical damage to his neck. He later revealed that this had been a suicide attempt. He had become overwhelmed and decided to ask for some help.

Although the officer had no indication that the detainee's condition had gotten so severe, he was relieved that no more damage had occurred than some dislocated vertebrae. The investigation that followed almost gave the officer as big a headache as the injured detainee.

There is considerable uneasiness and unrest in the population as a result of the incident. What happened?

1

What happened? First, we know that many detainees in a correctional setting are vulnerable. The cliché is of course true: "You do the crime, you do the time." There is another fact for officers: "And they are there for you to manage, FOR BETTER OR FOR WORSE." Being subjected to rigorous controls and forced to interact with many uneasy and even desperate human beings puts enormous pressures on inmates. When they act out uncontrollably, the person who is most vulnerable and available MAY BE YOU.

Second, we know that situations like the preceding one are not easily predicted. Inmates who may be mentally ill sometimes are responding to audio hallucinations. As hard as it is to understand, they hear voices that interfere at times and even seem to direct their behavior. At other times, the psychic pain becomes more than they can tolerate. Suicide seems irrational to most normal persons, but to someone whose life is constantly imposed on by severe depression or by intrusive voices or visions, suicide may unfortunately pose an escape. The officer who sizes up the situation and recognizes these symptoms will be more cautious and take these strange behaviors as symptoms of an illness just as they would a fever or complaints of physical pain.

Third, we must recognize that officers always have the option to handle a situation in a way that is for better—not worse. The officer in the above situation, for example, might have handled things in a different way. Can you think of one or two things he might have done to reduce the chances of the incident occurring? If so, list them below.

What could the officer have done?

1) _____

2) _____

2

Another example Let's consider another circumstance: An officer on the unit has a long list of names on his callout sheet. Inmates are heading in every direction—to a visit, to work detail, to the medical unit, to a meeting with the classification team, etc. The information is on a clipboard: names, assignments, times, etc. The officer is positioned beside the gate or door so that the detainees pass by in profile, giving only a side view.

After a few minutes, the officer's sheet is relatively clear and there is a lull before the next task. Then a detainee who had just left for a work detail appears and informs the officer that the lieutenant sent him back to the unit to change some clothes.

Hassles The inmate is written up by the correctional supervisor for wearing "free world" clothes. The duty officer is reprimanded by the shift lieutenant for the slip-up. The officer chews out the detainee for getting him into hot water with the lieutenant. No big deal—nothing like the earlier account of near tragedy. But look at all the hassle, the wasted energy! How do you think the duty officer might have acted to prevent this situation from arising? List one or two preventive actions below.

What could the duty officer have done?

1) _____

2) _____

Sizing things up In general, both of the officers in the previous accounts could have handled things better rather than worse if they had sized up the situation more accurately. The ability to do just this—to assess what's going on and decide what action should be taken—is perhaps the most critical part of any officer's job. Only the officer who really knows what's going on can choose and take the best possible course of action in managing detainees.

But "sizing up" is not an ability that an officer inherits. Nor is it always an ability that an officer develops through experience. After all, both of the officers in the above situations were quite experienced. Sizing things up requires some very definite skills. Perhaps you listed some of these skills in the answers that you gave. Or perhaps you drew a blank. By the time you finish with Section I, you'll not only have these skills, but will be able to put them to practical use in sizing up any situation.

What are the skills needed in sizing up?

THE FOUR
BASIC SKILLS

"Sizing up" any situation involves four very basic skills:

1) Positioning
2) Posturing
3) Observing
4) Listening

Why are they
considered
basic?

In the reading and exercises that follow, you'll have a chance to learn and practice each of these basic skills. The word *basic* is important. The four skill areas are basic and fundamental to everything you will learn in Sections II and III of this manual—and to everything you actually do on the job. You cannot hope to communicate safely and effectively with inmates until you have used these skills to size up the situation. Nor can you hope to control inmates unless you have first sized up the situation. On the other hand, by learning to make continual use of these four basic skills, you can maximize your chances of making the right response in situations where a wrong response could be very costly.

4

Use all the basics   The four basic skills are cumulative; each new skill builds on the previous one. For example, posturing yourself effectively means that you should already be in an appropriate position. Observing accurately means that you should have already gotten into an effective position and posture, and so on. You don't use one skill at a time. You size up a situation by making full use of all four basic skills.

Get ready to go on duty   The skilled officer always systematically sizes things up on each shift, whether responsible for work detail supervision or walking the tiers or ranges of a unit. Here are some ways an officer sizes things up before going on duty:

a) Checks with the supervisor and reviews the log book or the computer to see what has happened during the previous shift. If possible, is briefed by the officer being replaced.

b) Determines if there are items that need priority attention (like shaking down a recently vacated living area) and makes a note about taking care of them.

c) Walks the area of responsibility to take a reading on what is going on, who is where, and who is doing what, and to test the general atmosphere of the area.

d) Takes special note of any detainees identified as mentally ill and learns as much as possible about them.

It is in this final phase of pre-duty activity (and in the actual duty that follows) that the officer puts all four basic skills to maximum use.

5

Positioning

Physically position yourself in relation to an individual or a group. This is an extremely important skill in the effective management of inmates. Try listing one or two principles below that you feel might be important in terms of positioning.

What's important?

1) _____

2) _____

If you don't do these things, what might happen?

If I don't do these things...

1) _____

2) _____

If you do these things, what positive results might you get?

If I do them...

1) _____

2) _____

THREE STEPS OF POSITIONING

There are many different principles or activities that you may feel are important to effective positioning. The three major parts of positioning that we will focus on in this section are:

1) Establishing an appropriate distance
2) Facing squarely
3) Looking directly

At first these may seem obvious. But keep in mind the officer in the first account might have prevented a near tragedy had these skills been used when the inmate first approached him. And the other officer who was working with the call-out sheet might have avoided all the hassles if a better position had been taken.

As an effective officer, you need to position yourself where you can see and hear problems. Being in a good position helps you know what's going on and helps you avoid problems. In addition, inmates who think they are not being observed are always more of a problem because they tend to live by the rule "We'll get away with as much as we can—or as much as you let us."

As you know, it's impossible for you to be everywhere at once. It is also very difficult to catch inmates in certain acts because of "look-outs." Yet the more you use positioning skills to see and hear (when making rounds, for example), the less likely it is that the inmates will get involved in things that are against the rules.

Now let's take a look at the three steps in positioning.

STEP 1 OF POSITIONING

Distance yourself. The first principle of distancing is to keep it safe, and safety is foremost. It is not enough, however. You can be safely in your office while inmates are doing some pretty negative things, thus defeating the purpose of positioning. You need to be at a safe distance, but you must also be able to see and hear what is going on. Hearing is perhaps less important than seeing when your only objective is to size up the situation, but when you need to use your communication skills (Section II: The Add-Ons), you'll find it necessary to position yourself so that you can hear just as well as you can see.

Safety

Sight

Hearing

POSITIONING means **distancing** yourself far enough to be safe, close enough to see and hear.

Face squarely. Facing your "territory" squarely so that you can see it all at the same time gives you the most effective line of vision. Your left shoulder should be lined up with the left boundary line of the area you are watching. Your right shoulder should be lined up with the right boundary line of the area you are watching.

Try to see everything

When you move your head to either side so that your chin is right above either shoulder, you should be able to see the entire field you are responsible for.

POSITIONING means **facing** the **inmate or inmates squarely.**

Be unpredictable

Sometimes the sheer size of the area for which you are responsible (for example, a recreational area) makes it impossible to remain "squared" in one position. Rotate yourself so that by successive movements you will have squarely faced all the areas or people you are responsible for. In rotating, as in all behaviors, it is always **important to change the order in which you do things so that inmates are not able to predict your behavior.** At the same time, you must be thorough regardless of the pattern you employ. Facing fully helps you size up a situation. You can see best when you are directly facing inmates. When your goal is communicating with inmates (Section II), this also lets them know you are open to hearing them.

8

Look directly at the individual(s) or physical space. If you fail to look directly at the subject you are managing, you will not be on top of the situation, even if you are in the right position and are facing squarely. Looking directly at a group means looking at their eyes. When questioning inmates, you can pick up important clues by closely observing their eyes and facial expressions. However, do what you can to avoid getting into a staring contest, which might set someone off. Your direct look tells them that you mean business and are not threatened. Many inmates believe that a person who won't look you in the eyes is afraid of you.

Make eye
contact to
suggest strength.

POSITIONING means **looking directly**
at the area and person or people
you're managing.

Use eye
contact to
communicate

Making eye contact is often the best way to communicate interest. Inmates become aware of our efforts to make contact with them when they see us looking directly at their faces. Of course, looking directly at inmates will also provide you with valuable information about them. If an inmate keeps shifting his or her eyes while talking to you, the individual is either uncomfortable with you or uncomfortable with what is being said. This kind of information is important.

PRACTICE   Now here are some practice exercises that will help you master the steps in positioning as you work your next shift. Practice getting ready to size up the situation by positioning when you make your rounds through your unit.

Practice distancing yourself   If you are working a tier or a unit with cells, make sure you are far enough away from the cell so that you are not vulnerable. If you are on a tier above the first floor, you may be able to use the rail as a guide; about three feet is usually adequate. Self-defense experts believe an arm's length (about three feet) gives you an opportunity to fend off a first thrust.

Practice facing squarely

Practice looking directly at individuals and areas   After you have practiced walking a safe distance away from the cells, stop at each cell or cubicle and position yourself so that you can face squarely and see the entire area. The best position is about three feet away from the mid-point of the front of the area. After distancing yourself, make sure you are squared so that you have the best possible sight-lines. Law enforcement officers caution that if you are to be faced with a weapon, facing squarely should be amended.

What would you do at other times?   Most of you have other responsibilities and posts within the facility besides inmate living areas. Write down the name of one other post you are assigned to (e.g., recreation or dining room), how far away from the inmates you should stand, what you should face fully, and what you should look directly at.

Duty Station: _____

Best Distance: _____

Face What: _____

Look At: _____

More practice in positioning

Here is another positioning exercise: Bob is a detainee who calls to you as you pass his living area. He says he needs to talk to you. Picture the way you might position yourself to communicate to him that you are interested. Write down what you would be doing.

_____

_____

Practice positioning in order to communicate interest

Given your actions, do you think Bob would say *"This officer is interested in me?"* Ask yourself what a person would do physically to communicate interest to you. Would he stay away or move closer? Face you fully or sideways? Look at you directly or look down at the floor? The next couple of times an inmate or anybody you know attempts to communicate with you, try several of these approaches. Then either note in your mind or on paper which approaches produced a more positive response from the person. Also note or write down the things the other person did to make you believe his response was positive or negative. You can use a format like the one shown on the following page.

What I did to communicate interest:

1) _____

2) _____

3) _____

How the other person reacted:

1) _____

2) _____

3) _____

Inmates generate many excuses to explain why they are "closed" persons. Although a "closed" inmate is like a time bomb, you will have to decide if you want an inmate to be closed or open with you. That's your choice. Remember, you choose the amount of involvement with the inmate. If you do choose to be involved, positioning is the first step.

THE BASICS

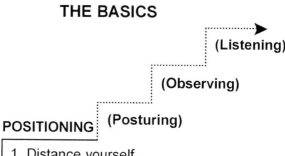

(Listening)

(Observing)

POSITIONING (Posturing)

1. Distance yourself
2. Face squarely
3. Look directly

Posturing

**THE SECOND
BASIC SKILL** Your posture—how you carry yourself—says a lot to an inmate. It can make an inmate think that you're confident of yourself and your abilities, or it can suggest that you're really pretty worried about what might happen. Your objective should be to show confidence. Try listing one or two posturing principles or activities that might show confidence.

**What's
important?** 1) _____

2) _____

What might happen if you don't do these things?

**If I don't do
these things...** 1) _____

2) _____

What do you think you will gain by doing these things?

If I do them... 1) _____

2) _____

**THREE STEPS
OF POSTURING** There are several steps involved in posturing when sizing up a situation. We'll focus on three:
1) Stand erect.
2) Eliminate distracting behaviors.
3) Incline yourself forward.

The way the first two procedures show confidence should be obvious. When you stand erect without distracting behaviors, you let inmates know that you're in full physical control—control not only of yourself but of the situation. This is essential. Many inmates will try to intimidate any officer who doesn't look as if she is confident about what she's doing. If an inmate thinks she can intimidate you, you're in real trouble. Any officer without the respect of inmates is open to manipulation and possible abuse. For example, there was an officer who was known to run at the first sign of trouble. Other officers felt insecure with him guarding the rear. He always stayed by the door of the dining room. But while the officers disliked this man, the inmates were all over him! They always managed to get what they wanted and still embarrass him. Finally he quit. Maybe you're thinking *"Fine—he shouldn't be an officer!"* But his case is just an extreme example of what happens when any officer gets pressured—or simply looks as though he or she could be intimidated.

By standing erect and eliminating distracting habits, you show your strength and confidence. The third step in posturing, inclining yourself forward, can also show confidence; it reinforces the idea that all your attention and potential energy is riveted on the inmate or inmates. Inclining yourself forward, as you will see in Section II, can also help communicate your interest. It says to the inmate, *I am inclined to listen, to pay attention, to be interested.*

Let's take a closer look at the three steps in posturing.

14

STEP 1 OF POSTURING	**Stand erect.** Each of you knows how important it is to stand straight and erect. You probably heard it as a child, and you definitely heard it if you served in the armed services: *Stand to your full height! Be proud! Stand up straight! Stick out that chest! Pull in that gut!* Standing erect takes muscle tone and practice. Look in the mirror and check yourself out: Are your shoulders straight? Is your chest caved in? How do you feel? Ask someone else for his reaction. Which way makes you look stronger and more confident?
Strength	
Confidence	

POSTURING means **standing erect**
to show strength and confidence.

STEP 2 OF POSTURING	**Eliminate distracting behaviors.** A person not standing steady is seen as insecure. Nail biting, foot tapping, and other distracting behaviors do not communicate confidence and control, but standing stiff like a board doesn't communicate it either. You should not feel tension in your body when you stand, once you have stopped distracting behaviors.
Control	

POSTURING means **eliminating all
distracting behaviors.**

STEP 3 OF POSTURING	**Incline forward.** Your intention here must be to communicate interest and concern by shifting your weight forward so that the inmates become more aware of your "inclination" to communicate and supervise them with respect. You can do this by placing one foot a little in front of the other and putting your weight on the forward foot. This communicates "moving closer" without actually moving you much closer or making any physical contact. This
Show interest and concern	

15

position shows that you are more alert, and it gives you more control over the situation. Lean your weight away from the other person for a moment: What do you experience? Probably a "laid back" sort of remoteness. You're simply not as involved.

POSTURING means **inclining yourself forward** to show that your attention is really focused.

When you have correctly positioned yourself, your posture gives the initial message of your intent. By keeping your distance and by standing fully erect, you have given clear signals. By moving closer and by inclining yourself toward the inmate, you signal to the inmate that you will be giving him or her your full attention. If the inmate has requested that attention, your posture tells him that you are interested in what is being said. If you initiated the move without being directly asked, however, the message may not be clear. The inmate may be thinking *"Oh, oh, what now?"* They will need other facial and/or verbal cues before realizing your intent.

As you begin your positioning skills to use, practice your **posturing** skills. Once you have the most effective position, stand erect and make sure you've eliminated distracting behaviors. Then incline your body very slightly forward toward the inmate or group you wish to observe. You've begun to use the first two of the four basic skills involved in sizing up the situation.

By assuming an effective position and posture, you are ready for maximum input—ready, that is, for the information you need in order to size up the situation fully and accurately. Observing and listening are the skills you can use to get the necessary input.

16

During correctional management, a poorly positioned and postured officer is vulnerable. He communicates, for any number of reasons, that he doesn't want to be there with the inmate. Talking to someone who doesn't want to be there doesn't reinforce an inmate to do what he is supposed to do. In fact, it might make him think about taking advantage.

Practice identifying distractions Can you think of some of your own behaviors that are distracting? How about distracting behaviors you have observed in others?

1) _____

2) _____

What message does it send?

_____

_____

What makes it distracting?

_____

_____

Practice skills together The next time an inmate initiates what you believe to be a genuine request, put together the steps of positioning and posturing for effective management.

What do they do? What is the reaction as you begin to focus your attention?

_____

_____

Is the reaction negative, or is it positive?

_____

_____

Why do you think so (e.g., does the detainee move closer to you or further away)?

_____

_____

When you practice positioning (distancing, squaring, looking directly) in the units and at other posts, practice standing erect and eliminating distracting behaviors. If you feel confident in the situation, position yourself for inmate management and show a few distracting behaviors, but don't stand straight. What is the reaction of the inmates?

_____

_____

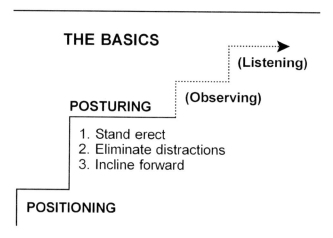

THE BASICS   ....➤
                                  (Listening)

POSTURING   **(Observing)**

   1. Stand erect
   2. Eliminate distractions
   3. Incline forward

POSITIONING

Observing

THE THIRD
BASIC SKILL Since what we observe is more likely to tell us what we need to know than words, it's obviously important for an officer to observe inmates. But what does "observation" really mean? List a couple of very basic things you would want to look for while observing any inmate or group of inmates.

What's important?

1) _____

2) _____

What kinds of things can you learn by observing these basic things?

If I do this...

1) _____

2) _____

Finally, what risks might there be in not observing these things?

If I don't do this...

1) _____

2) _____

Observing the inmate effectively requires the officer to notice and understand inmate behavior, appearance, and environment. Negative examples of inmate behavior might be an inmate looking at the floor as you go by, or turning away from you. A "positive" inmate might be one who always follows directions without back-talk. A "neutral" inmate might be one who does just enough to get along—no hassles but no real cooperation either. By observing inmate behavior, appearance, and environment, you can find out which inmates might cooperate with you and which inmates might hold back or even pose a threat. By failing to observe these basic things, of course, you risk missing out on possible cooperation and may even put yourself in physical danger without realizing it.

You get information

Where inmates really are

What they might do

Simply stated, observing gives you information about an inmate's state of mind in relation to the institution's expectations. Effective observing allows you to check out and confirm an inmate's intentions. Knowing where an inmate is and what he or she plans to do will allow you to anticipate problems and act to control them before there is any trouble. Not only will close observation of an inmate give you information about his intentions, but it will also allow you to use that knowledge to detect changes in inmate attitude and behavior. Noticing and understanding changes in inmate behavior are critical parts of managing behavior. When you know an inmate, you can act accordingly; but if you miss a change in behavior, it could lead to problems—even tragedy.

Example

For example, Patty was a pretty decent inmate who was constructively involved in her unit. An officer observed that Patty was staying more to herself and was sleeping more. This alert officer initiated a talk with her. It turned out that Patty was not taking her medicine as prescribed; she had not been swallowing and later spitting it in the commode. Her paranoia led her to believe that the medication was evil. With the support of her unit officer and the nurse's intervention, she was soon back on track.

Another example

In another situation, an officer observed a small group of inmates who appeared agitated and restless. He reduced the distance between himself and the group, positioned himself so

20

that he could make more accurate observations, and discovered that the group was planning to do some "vigilante" work on another inmate who had been using sexual intimidation on some younger inmates. The officer discovered who they were talking about and arranged for a transfer of the inmate in question, thereby averting a possible violent encounter.

What to observe Observing really means focusing on three things: behavior, appearance, and environment.

Behavior A **behavior** is a nonverbal cue that comes from something that the inmate does consciously and actively. For example, an officer might observe any or all of the following behaviors: two inmates holding hands; an inmate going out of his way to bump another inmate; an inmate quietly reading, another wringing her hands.

Appearance An **appearance** is a nonverbal cue that an inmate might display even if unconscious or dead. For example, an officer might observe the following "appearances": one inmate is tattooed; another inmate didn't wear clean clothes today; a third inmate is an older person.

Environment **Environment** refers to the specific people and things that an inmate has around him or her in a particular place.

FOUR STEPS OF OBSERVING In addition to basic positioning and posturing, **observing** involves these four steps:

1) Look at inmate behavior, appearance, and environment.

2) Draw inferences about the inmate's feelings, relationships with staff and others, energy level, and values.

3) Decide whether what you see is normal or abnormal for a given inmate.

4) Determine the implications for management (Trouble? No trouble?).

The term *inference* as used here simply means drawing tentative conclusions as to the meaning or significance of something, based on your experience with similar inmate behaviors, appearances, or environments. It may reflect knowledge gained in training or from other officers.

By mastering the skills of positioning and posturing, you have made a start on learning to observe individuals, groups, and environments. As indicated earlier, you cannot observe any inmate or group of inmates unless you are in a good physical position to do so. You should be far enough away so that you are not vulnerable and so that you can take in the entire scene by moving nothing more than your head. At the same time, you should be close enough to pick up on those visual cues concerning inmate behavior, appearance, and environment that will tell you what is happening.

STEP 1 OF OBSERVING

Look at behavior, appearance, and environment. As you have already learned, it is important to look directly at the inmate or group you are observing. Sure, it's important for officers to be able to pick up on things out of the corner of their eyes, such as a sudden movement that might signal an attack. The fact remains, however, that we see people or things most clearly when we are looking right at them. When you observe an inmate, try to answer mental questions such as *What's she doing right now?* (behavior); *What are the important things about how she looks?* The detainee is sitting quietly but has elevated her legs on another chair. You look closely and notice

What's she doing?

How does she look?

22

Where is she? And with whom?	swelling in her calves. *What's important about where she is and who she's with?* (environment). Once you're able to answer these questions, you're ready to draw some inferences.

OBSERVING means looking at inmate behavior, appearance, and environment.

STEP 2 OF OBSERVING	**Draw inferences.** Inferences are the initial conclusions you come to as the result of observing inmates. You take in visual cues related to inmate appearance, behavior, and environment. These cues are really "clues" that show you something about inmate feelings, relationships, energy levels, and values. The more observations you make, the more inferences you can draw—and the more accurate these inferences will be.

OBSERVING means drawing inferences about inmate feelings, relationships, energy levels, and values.

Remember the inmate with the swollen legs? What hunch do you have? Detainees on neuroleptic medicines often have side effects.

Drawing inferences about feelings	The officer uses observing skills to draw inferences about how an individual inmate or an entire unit of inmates is feeling. Knowing how an individual is feeling is critical in determining where a person is emotionally. For example, you might use the word *happy* to describe an
How does he probably feel?	inmate who is exercising and smiling. For an inmate who is pacing while wringing his hands, you might use the word *tense.* You might use the term *uptight* to describe a group of inmates who are tightly clustered and talking in a well-guarded, hesitant manner.

What "feeling" word would you apply to the following examples?

a) An inmate is sitting on her bed with her head down, slowly rocking back and forth.

Feeling word:

_____

b) A detainee is holding a picture. He is pointing to it while standing erect. Now he pauses to show it to you. He has tears in his eyes; the picture is of a small child.

Feeling word:

_____

Drawing inferences about relationships

Is he positive, negative, or neutral about others?

Besides being aware of the nonverbal cues that indicate the feelings of the inmate, the officer can further increase effectiveness in correctional management by looking for cues that indicate the nature of the relationship between himself and the inmates and between inmates themselves. These relationships serve as good indicators of future action. An inmate who has a good relationship with an officer may provide valuable information about potential breaks in security. An inmate who has a bad relationship with either an officer or another inmate may be a source of violence. Consider the inmate who was originally sentenced to five years. He really doesn't like certain types of inmates and it shows. He has now been in prison for sixteen years because of assaults on other inmates.

In general, you can categorize relationships and feelings as **positive, negative,** or **neutral.** Inmates who do things to make your job easier (e.g., arrive on time) probably have or want to have a positive relationship with you. An inmate who always tries to hassle you (e.g.,

24

uses abusive language, refuses to obey orders) doesn't have a positive relationship with you and doesn't want one.

Examples Among inmates, relationships of power are critical. Usually inmates form their own group and select a leader. Knowing the relationship within and between groups is crucial. For example, a bumping between members of different groups can mean real trouble. In addition, homosexual relationships, drug relationships, and gambling relationships are potential sources of great problems. You might observe that two inmates who have a close relationship are no longer hanging together. You might further observe that one of the inmates is with some new inmate. This could mean a problem is brewing.

PRACTICE Write down two behaviors and/or appearances that suggest that two inmates have a negative relationship.

_____

_____

Write down what might result from these behaviors and/or appearances.

_____

Write down two behaviors and/or appearances that suggest that two inmates have a positive relationship.

_____

_____

Write down what might result from these behaviors and/or appearances.

_____

_____

25

Write down two behaviors and/or appearances that suggest that an inmate feels positive toward you.

_____

_____

Write down what might result from these behaviors and/or appearances.

_____

_____

Write down two behaviors and/or appearances that suggest that an inmate feels negative toward you.

_____

_____

Write down what might result from these behaviors and/or appearances.

_____

_____

Drawing inferences about energy level

Energy: high? low? medium?

Energy level tells us a great deal about how much and what type of trouble an inmate can and/or will cause. For example, inmates with a **low** energy level tend to be reluctant to initiate anything. Many inmates have a low energy level: They look and act defeated, their movements are slow, and their heads hang down. Every move seems like an effort to these inmates, who will probably spend a good part of their time sleeping. Inmates with **moderate** energy levels actively engage in most activities (playing cards, talking, eating), while **high** energy inmates participate in all that is required, but also make use of physical fitness equipment, and engage in other optional activities. The danger of high energy, of course, is that this energy needs to be used constructively so that it does not

26

become a source of danger. In general, it is important to keep all inmates occupied and involved in activities, but with high-energy types, it is absolutely essential.

While it is important to observe basic levels of energy, changes in energy level are even more critical. An inmate's energy level is usually constant except at special times (e.g., visiting hours). Changes from high to low or low to high can indicate trouble (such as drugs or imminent violence to self or others), or can indicate potential mental illness.

PRACTICE Can you think of two things that an individual's energy level tells you about that person?

_____

_____

Write down two ways in which energy level relates to your job duties.

_____

_____

Write down two special times that might cause inmate energy levels to change.

_____

_____

Drawing inferences about values It is also important to understand what a given inmate values. Observing the inmate's environment provides important clues. Every inmate has basic environments: some examples might be the living unit, a work unit (kitchen), and possibly a learning unit (school). In each of these **Who does the inmate run with?** settings, the "environment" will include not only physical materials, but people—the individuals whom the inmate "runs with." You can learn a great deal about an inmate by carefully observing his or her "environment." A general rule is, what a person gives energy to is a value; the more energy, the higher the value. However, energy given is not a perfect measure, but it is significant. For example, a person might value good health, but do **nothing** to maintain or achieve it.

What interests the inmate? Your observations should help you find out how the inmate relates to his or her environment. Does this person have friends? Who are they? Remember, birds of a feather definitely do flock together! A detainee who hangs out with a drug crowd is telling you something. What is important to the inmate? Look for things in the environment that reflect the inmate's interests and values (Is her cell neat? What does he read? and so on). Knowing what an inmate values has real implications for effective management. When you know what a detainee wants (and doesn't want), you've got an edge in managing that detainee. When you understand an inmate's values, interests, friends, etc., you understand that inmate's culture within the institution. Cultures establish the rules and behaviors that will be reinforced. People want to belong to a culture; it offers security even though it may be deviant. Gangs or gang affiliation are examples on the street as well as in "the joint."

What risks are there in the setting? There is also the obvious matter of risk in certain environments. Each setting has its own unique set of dangers that must be understood. In a kitchen, an inmate can easily find a weapon. Knowing an inmate's normal "life style" as reflected in the environment can help you anticipate problems or dangers arising from a particular inmate being in a particular setting. One inmate's behavior, appearance, and the way he relates to his environment might signal the real value he places on direct and often

28

violent physical action. This inmate would be a particular risk in any setting where tools of violence can be found.

PRACTICE List five things (in relation to environment) that might reflect inmate values. Then pick two inmates and see if you can observe these things and values. For example, you might observe an inmate exercising and infer that he values physical fitness and/or appearance.

Five things that reflect inmate values

1) _____

2) _____

3) _____

4) _____

5) _____

Reasons should be observable and concrete The reasons for your inferences should be visual cues related to behaviors, appearances, and environment. Inferences stand the best chance of being accurate if they are based on detailed and concrete observations as opposed to vague and general ones. A detailed and concrete observation will help prevent being fuzzy, will lead to more accurate conclusions, and will receive fuller attention from those who are listening.

Example For example, consider this observation: "I saw a group of inmates giving another inmate a hard time after visiting hours." Now consider this second observation: "I saw a group of five large inmates approach a new, young inmate who is slightly built. They went up to him and started waving their arms. One of them put his arm around the young inmate's neck and shoulder and pulled him abruptly to him while looking him

29

in the face. The young inmate grimaced and tried to pull away. The larger inmates laughed, and after a few more minutes, one inmate appeared to get the group to break up." The second observation is a much more useful description of what has happened. You have just possibly witnessed a classic example of a "boo game." The young detainee may now "belong" to the detainee who rescued him.

PRACTICE From the second observation, can you identify how the younger, smaller inmate felt? Try to identify his relationship to the other inmates (positive, negative, neutral), and gauge his energy level (high, medium, low). State your reason.

He was feeling: _____
(angry, scared, happy, sad)

Reason why you think this:

_____

Relationship with other inmates: _____
(positive/negative)

Energy level: _____
(high, moderate, low)

STEP 3 OF OBSERVING **Decide whether things are normal or abnormal.** Once you've been on the job for a while, you get to know how individual inmates tend to function. One individual is easygoing and hardly ever hassles with others. A second always looks mad at the world. A third always seems to be feeling self-pity. Your observations and the

Normal? inferences you've drawn can help you determine

Abnormal? whether a particular inmate is in a "normal" or an "abnormal" condition at any point in time.

OBSERVING means determining if things are normal or abnormal.

In determining whether things are normal or abnormal for a given inmate at a given time, compare your present observations of the inmate with what you have seen in the past and/or with comments other officers have made about the inmate. For example, you might see an inmate arguing loudly with another inmate— he might even be making threats of one kind or another. If this is normal behavior for this inmate, you probably need to exercise only the usual amount of caution. But if the appearance and the behavior of the angry inmate are highly unusual or abnormal for him, you'll know it's a potentially violent situation. Getting to know detainees is essential in establishing standards for normal and abnormal.

PRACTICE Choose two inmates with whom you're familiar—ones you've had a chance to observe over a period of time. Then list one or two "normal" features of their behavior, appearance, and environment and one or two "abnormal" features that might tip you off to a possible management problem. Even though mentally ill detainees are considered abnormal to society, you will learn their patterns and establish normal for them. Having auditory hallucinations is "normal" for some of them. Surprisingly, once you understand their "abnormality/normality" **you** may understand. Some individuals believe that people who work in corrections to be abnormal themselves. But we know differently... don't we?

31

INMATE #1

Normal behavior: _____

Normal appearance: _____

Normal environment: _____

Abnormal behavior: _____

Abnormal appearance: _____

Abnormal environment: _____

INMATE #2

Normal behavior: _____

Normal appearance: _____

Normal environment: _____

Abnormal behavior: _____

Abnormal appearance: _____

Abnormal environment: _____

STEP 4 OF
OBSERVING

Trouble?
No trouble?

Decide whether there is trouble or no trouble. This decision should be based on your observations and your knowledge of detainee life. With your knowledge of detainee life and life in general, you should be able to generate certain principles that will be useful when coupled with your observations in making this decision. For example:

- Birds of a feather flock together.

- A very depressed person usually withdraws from activities and other people.

- When 10 to 15 percent of a group of inmates are down, tense, or hostile, it can affect the entire group.

- Abrupt and/or major changes in behavior and/or appearance mean trouble.

- A guy who has used a shank before has a greater likelihood of doing it again.

OBSERVING means **determining whether a situation is "trouble" or "no trouble."**

Example   For example, consider the situation where you observe a homosexual with a different mate than the one with whom he had been keeping company. The homosexual's former partner has been shouting at you and others lately, staying up at night, and you have also seen him following his old partner and the new person. Given these observations, you can infer that the inmate is angry (shouting), has a negative relationship with his old partner (he is no longer with this partner), and his energy level is up (not sleeping and following the new couple around). You combine these inferences with your knowledge that inmates do harm inmates when a sexual relationship breaks down this way. And you know that the first partner is probably going to get even with this new partner for, among other things, a poor image (losing his partner). You decide that this is a trouble situation.

33

PRACTICE For practice, size up inmates in a unit by using your positioning, posturing, and observing skills. Label each situation or person as "trouble" or "no trouble." Position and posture yourself so that you can manage effectively. Observe the inmates, and use this information to draw inferences about feelings, relationships, values, and energy level. Decide whether things are "normal" or "abnormal." Then use your observations and any other knowledge or principles you have to decide if the individual or situation is "trouble" or "no trouble." After you finish your rounds, try to write down all of this so that you can review it later. Think of the exercise in the following way:

You see: _____

You infer: (feelings) _____

(relationships) _____

(energy level) _____

(values) _____

You determine: (normal or abnormal)

_____

You decide: (trouble or no trouble)

_____

In addition to the above exercise, pick two other settings in which you work or have worked and write down the behaviors and/or appearances that would indicate trouble in that setting. Make sure you give your reasons.

Observe before you communicate

Observing inmate appearance and behavior is usually the quickest and most accurate way to detect whether a given individual is really having a problem. Don't count on someone telling you: Inmates are usually reluctant to talk about problems. Your observations will allow you to anticipate problems. This way, you can prepare for any possible impact on the individual inmate, on other inmates, and even on you and other officers. In general, the steps in observing for possible communication purposes are the same as those that you take in observing for risks. The only major change is that you must ask about the implications for your involvement. Should you or should you not communicate (get involved) with an inmate based on your observations of the inmate's appearance and behavior, and the inferences you have drawn concerning the inmate's feelings, his or her relationship with you and others, and his or her general energy level?

Get involved?
Not get involved?

PRACTICE

Feeling?
Relationship?
Energy?
Reason?
Knowledge?
Decision?

Read over the following situation and use the space provided to identify the inmate's feelings, relationship to the officer, and energy level. Give reasons for your inference (behaviors, appearances, and any knowledge and/or principles that apply). Finally, decide whether the officer should become involved with the inmate by communicating with him or her.

An inmate is lying in bed in sort of a fetal position. You hear what you believe to be moaning, but as you move closer it sounds more like humming. There is no evidence of pain, etc. The detainee continues for that way for a few seconds, then jumps up and moves rapidly to the door. He grabs the ledge of the small opening in the door and leans on it for a few minutes. All the while he is leaning on the door, he just stares blankly out into space. As you approach the door, the inmate jumps back and quickly returns to his bed. The officer says *"Hi, John,"* but the inmate neither looks at the officer nor says anything. After the officer moves away, the inmate again jumps out of bed and returns to the door.

Feeling _____ + Reason _____

Relationship to
Officer _____ + Reason _____

Energy
Level _____ + Reason _____

Any principles
that apply: _____

Involvement?
No involvement? _____ + Reason _____

PRACTICE   List three problem areas that inmates have and indicate what the symptoms (behaviors, appearances) of those problems usually are. For **Problem?** instance, suicide is a problem area in a very **Symptom?** broad sense: The act itself might be the result of a variety of particular problems, such as the loss of a loved one or loneliness. An inmate contemplating suicide feels extremely depressed, disappointed, hopeless, or afraid, and is usually under a lot of pressure. He might have bags under his eyes because he hasn't slept. He'll probably have physical symptoms, such as cuts on his arm or bruises around his neck. Other clues: attempts to store up pills, not opening his mail, refusing to eat, and losing weight. List three problem areas below, as well as their symptoms:

1) Problem _____ Symptom _____

2) Problem _____ Symptom _____

3) Problem _____ Symptom _____

Make sure you know what to observe in inmates—and *what your observations really mean*—before you move on to the next section on **listening.**

THE BASICS

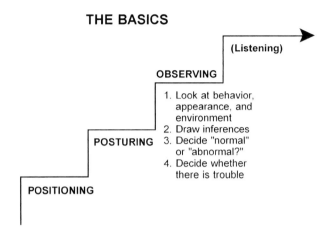

(Listening)

OBSERVING

1. Look at behavior, appearance, and environment
2. Draw inferences

POSTURING

3. Decide "normal" or "abnormal?"
4. Decide whether there is trouble

POSITIONING

Listening

Like observing, listening is clearly an important skill for officers. All too often, however, it's the kind of activity that is taken for granted: *"Yeah, sure, I keep my ears open."* But there's more to listening than just keeping the ears open! Try listing one or two basic procedures that you believe skilled listening involves:

**What's
important?**

1) _____

2) _____

What might you learn if you followed these procedures?

If I do this...

1) _____

2) _____

What problems might arise if you don't bother to follow these procedures?

**If I don't do
this...**

1) _____

2) _____

**FOUR STEPS
OF LISTENING** Perhaps you listed the basic skills of Positioning, Posturing, and Observing as important things an officer must do before he or she can really listen effectively. If so, you're absolutely right—although it's not always possible to observe an inmate all the time, you're listening to what he's saying.

But the skill of listening involves more than these three basic procedures plus "keeping your ears open." You must also **suspend your personal judgment** (only temporarily, of course); **pick out key words; identify the intensity** of an inmate's communication; and **determine the particular mood.**

38

Look for verbal cues and signals Inmates often go through a verbal stage before the action begins. If you can hear the danger signals, you can cut off trouble before it breaks out. Listening involves the officer's ability to hear and accurately recall all the important verbal cues used by the inmates. "Important" here means stated or implied signals of trouble or problems. The danger may be an inmate's intention to harm him- or herself or another inmate, or his or her intention to inflict harm on an officer. You can listen for cues that mean violence may occur or that violence is possible if preventive action is not taken. For example, an officer hears an unusual noise coming from the shower area. When he investigated, an inmate was attempting suicide by jamming a towel into a shutoff on the shower wall.

Other important cues: verbal threats ("I'm gonna get that mother_____!"), strong statements of desire or need about people on the outside ("I'm gonna go crazy if I can't get out and see my old lady!"), and statements about things like gambling debts ("He owes me, man—he owes me!"). Complaints from inmates are common, of course, but they're also very important. The most effective officers listen to complaints and recognize when a familiar cue is uttered in a new tone, or when a complaint arises from a usually uncomplaining inmate. Listen for changes: silence when there is usually noise (dining area) or noise when there is usually silence (3:00 a.m. in the cell block). Ask yourself this question: *Is there trouble here?*

Get ready to listen Get ready to listen by using the basic positioning, posturing, and observing skills. A good position will obviously help you hear better. Posturing, while perhaps less important in terms of listening for management, is essential when you're listening to an inmate who really wants to talk to you. Your posture can signal that you're focusing all your attention on him.

Position

Posture

Observe

39

Finally, your observing skills cannot always be used to promote better listening—for example, you may overhear something that inmates are talking about around a corner. But when possible, visual observations help you understand the implications of what you're hearing. An inmate who sounds angry but turns out to be leaning back in his chair and grinning may have only been telling a story to others; an inmate whose angry voice fits with his tense, up-tight appearance presents quite a different situation.

Concentrate
Don't expect to be able to listen effectively to an inmate if you've got other things on your mind. If you're thinking about home or other job responsibilities, you might miss a lot. You've got to focus on the inmate to whom you're listening—and this takes a good deal of concentration. You can work to develop this kind of concentration by reviewing what you're going to do and whom you're going to see before you assume your post. Then you'll be ready to start using the four skills of listening. One of our greatest philosophers, Lee Trevino, said *"The more I practice... the luckier I get."*

STEP 1 OF LISTENING

Don't pre-judge

Listen for all the cues

Suspend judgment. This is very difficult to do because society has already passed judgment on the inmate. Yet most officers agree that it's important to judge a person on what he or she does *now*, inside the facility, rather than on what he or she did on the outside. It is still hard at times to listen without making an immediate judgment: After all, most inmates complain about other inmates, the institution, and you, or they demand to be given something. However, you won't be effective in corrections management unless you suspend judgment, because when you pre-judge, you will not hear the real verbal cues you need to pick up on to prevent danger or assist someone.

40

> **LISTENING** means **suspending your own judgment** temporarily so that you can hear what's being said.

All complaints sound the same after a while—but they are not! Some are just the normal negatives of inmates while others are warning signs. Just let the inmate's message sink in before making any decisions about it. Of course, certain situations call for quick action; but if you develop your non-judgmental listening ability now, you will hear better and will be able to judge and act more quickly when necessary.

STEP 2 OF LISTENING

Pick out key words. Listen for key words and phrases, and add some of your own. Here are a few: *kill, depressed, snitch, honky, waste, hawk, crow, nigger, blackman.* Listen for these

Key words phrases also: *You'll pay. Get out of here! Hostage.* Of course, everything you hear and see must be considered in terms of who the inmate is that did or said it. (Some inmates are always threatening and sounding off.) In addition to the key words, you'll need to identify the person who is involved.

> **LISTENING** means **picking out key words and phrases** like *get* or *shank* or *that sissy.*

Because asking questions is so important, we introduce it here and then review it again in the Add-Ons where we will introduce and practice communication skills. The formula for asking useful questions is the 5WH method. It stands for **Who, What, When, Where, Why,** and **How.** Answers to these questions tell you important things you need to know.

41

Who's talking?

Who's being talked about?

Here's a quick exercise. One inmate told another, *"That Ralph owes me twelve dollars since day one. I told him to come across, but he said, 'No way—take it out of my butt.' Well, that's just what I'm going to do. I'll get that mother. Who does he think he's messing with!"*

PRACTICE

Now pick out what you believe to be the key words and phrases. Write the four most important ones below. Use the 5WHs as your guide.

1. Key word: _____

   Reason: _____

   _____

2. Key word: _____

   Reason: _____

   _____

3. Key word: _____

   Reason: _____

   _____

4. Key word: _____

   Reason: _____

   _____

Certainly one key word here would be *get.* Another is *Ralph,* the name of the person involved. As it turned out, the inmate did cut Ralph. Ralph needed 42 stitches to close the wounds. Inmates are very careful about what they say near an officer, yet they often do give preliminary verbal cues openly enough to be detected.

STEP 3 OF LISTENING

Volume?
Emotion?
Intensity:
high? medium?
low?

Identify intensity. Statements are made with varying intensity (high, moderate, and low). The louder and more emotional a statement, the more intense it is. But loudness and emotion are not the same thing. A wavering voice, for example, signals a lot of emotion even though it may not be loud. A statement that is either loud or emotional but not both is of moderate intensity. A statement that is not loud and is empty of emotion is of low intensity. High intensity statements are very real signs of danger. You can see the importance of getting to know detainees well as soon as possible. Often it's the deviation from the way persons are as you normally experience them that determines the perception of intensity.

LISTENING means **determining whether the intensity of an inmate's speech is high, medium, or low.**

STEP 4 OF LISTENING

Is the mood positive, negative, or neutral?

Reflect on what the mood is and why. Reflect on the mood to determine whether it is positive, negative, or neutral and normal or abnormal. Mood here means what the inmates are feeling. One question you may ask to determine mood is "What kinds of feelings are being expressed or implied (positive, negative, neutral)?" Another question you want to answer is "Is this mood normal or abnormal for this time and place for this detainee?" Sure, there are always exceptions. A detainee may say *"I'm going to kill you,"* quietly and without emotion yet still mean it. This is why it is so important to know your detainees and to continue to observe and listen for other cues.

43

LISTENING means **determining whether an inmate's mood is positive, neutral, or negative** and whether this mood is **normal** or **abnormal.**

Reasons When you answer the question *"Is this normal or abnormal?"* try to formulate the reason why this is the case. "Normal" means as it usually is. This can apply to one inmate as well as to a large group of inmates. Inmates are usually consistent in their behaviors in the various settings of the institution. For example, it's not normal for inmates to be really up when they are not occupied; therefore, if your inmates are flying when there are no visiting hours due, no work, no shop, etc., then things are not normal and the possibility of danger exists.

PRACTICE Think of two situations that are typical of prison life. Describe the normal mood and give sample verbal cues (what inmates say) that suggest that the mood is not normal. Give the reason you might have for thinking it is not normal. For example, you might describe one situation as "inmates in their cell." The normal mood of these inmates at this particular time might be calm and relaxed. But now you find them talking crudely. Their mood is negative and definitely abnormal for them. Your reasons for making a determination of the mood might be key words you hear, such as *waste* or phrases such as *that fink Jimbo* uttered in loud and angry tones.

SITUATION #1

Normal mood: _____

Present mood: _____

Your reasons: _____

SITUATION #2

Normal mood: _____

Present mood: _____

Your reasons: _____

PRACTICE   As a way of further practicing your listening skills, list the key words and/or phrases from the following dialogue. Do you think any of them mean trouble? Why? Write out your reasons.

John: *"I know Larry is a snitch, because I saw him talking to Officer Brown right before Brown made his rounds."*

Mike: *"Well, he really cost us a lot of stuff. We really got on with it the last few nights. Now half of the stuff's gone, and James has been busted out of here."*

Jim: *"We need to pay Larry a visit and get his head straight."*

John: *"Not right away, or the 'hacks' will be sure to know it's about the stuff last night. Let it go for a couple of weeks. Then we nail him."*

Jim: *"What about Officer Brown? You see how he treated James—like dirt. I'd like to get him, too."*

Key phrases: _____

_____

Trouble? ❑ Yes   ❑ No   Your reasons:

_____

_____

When you get to your main post, try to identify the mood of the setting and the reasons for your identification. Classify the mood as normal or abnormal. In the other settings you find yourself in, listen for the typical management problems in that setting. Are there places where it is easier to overhear an inmate discussing or participating in a breach of management? If yes, where?

PRACTICE You should be able to recall all the important parts of conversations you hear, especially when an inmate is talking right to you. Check out your ability by summarizing the content of the following paragraph:

> *"I can't go back to work anymore. The supervisor has it in for me. I know I'm heading for trouble, and I don't want any. My record is clean. I obey all the rules. This guy, he doesn't care about all that. He says I don't do my work. That's bull! Ask any other inmate. I may not fall over when he tells me what to do, but I always do it. I don't talk back or nothing. I don't want to blow it, but he is really making me look stupid and then he laughs about it. Even the other guys are picking up on it. It's real bad; you gotta help me."*

Your summary: _____

_____

_____

_____

_____

_____

46

When you return to your post, practice summarizing an inmate's statement. Can you classify the types of problems you get in each of the settings?

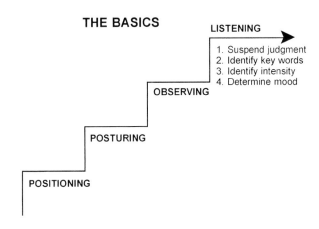

THE BASICS

LISTENING

1. Suspend judgment
2. Identify key words
3. Identify intensity
4. Determine mood

OBSERVING

POSTURING

POSITIONING

Now, what have you learned?

It hasn't been that long since Sherry finished her training and started on the job as a correctional officer. Her lack of experience really didn't bother her too much, however. She had a lot going for her. For one thing, she had some good basic skills.

She walked the unit early in her shift. At one table, two detainees played cards, their usual game. She'd watched them before. They'd play for an hour—no more, no less. All part of their own routine. So long as they stuck to it, Sherry knew things were all right.

At another table, an inmate was reading. Another detainee, named Sandra, paced the unit near her room. Tension there—Sandra was usually a quiet, relaxed person. Sherry remembered the nurse had said Sandra's illness was called bi-polar disorder and that she might have wide fluctuations in her mood: depressed then even hyperactive. Better keep a close eye and report her observation to the nurse. No problem yet, but she wanted to be ahead of anything.

Sherry had a lot going for her with her basic skills. And now you have the same skills to work for you: being able to minimize risk and maximize your effectiveness on the job. Being a correctional officer is never easy. But it's near impossible if all you have to go on is impulse and the mythology about detainee management. Now you can move beyond limited capabilities and start to put some real professionalism into your work.

Summary of the Basics

You've had a chance to learn the four basic skills you need to size up a situation to manage your job and the inmates more effectively. You practiced **positioning, posturing, observing,** and **listening.** But as you know, there's far more to being an effective officer than being able to size things up. There will be times when you will choose to manage by communicating with inmates. You'll want to defuse a troublesome situation or get important information. Or you may want to get involved with an inmate's concerns.

In Section II, we'll consider the skills you'll need to communicate with inmates. They are optional when it comes to helping inmates with personal problems, but they are absolutely essential when dealing with tense situations—situations where strong feelings can and will spin out of control unless you're able to communicate with inmates. Sizing things up just lets you know what's happening or what might happen. To change things for the better (and that's what effective management requires), you need to add communication skills to your management toolkit.

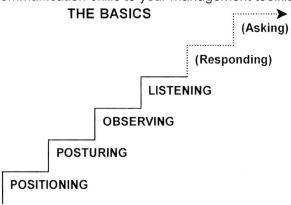

THE BASICS

(Asking)

(Responding)

LISTENING

OBSERVING

POSTURING

POSITIONING

Section II

The Add-Ons:
Communicating with Inmates

Example   **What's it all about?**

One detention facility had, as most do, a special unit for detainees whose freedom was tightly restricted because of in-house infractions, fighting, insubordination, etc. As tight as security was within this unit, a special cell within it housed inmates who were especially difficult to manage. It was placed directly across from the duty station of two officers. One was at a podium on the first floor of the unit, another in a special room bordered by bullet proof glass and always locked. Detainees were observed 24/7 by two officers who rotated during the shift.

A smallish Latino detainee was the present guest in the special cell. He was the most distractive detainee ever to occupy the cell. He had to be escorted even within the unit: shackled, cuffed, etc. It took three or four officers to ready him to meet with detention officials. He was mentally ill and had medicines prescribed, but compliance was a major issue. He was creative with his urine and feces. His water was frequently turned off for obvious reasons. He frequently cried out and held ongoing arguments with inmates.

The other inmates in the unit were exhausted by his clamor. Officers often resorted to unethical tactics to quiet him down. They would leave his intercom on at night, hoping to wear him down. When it was necessary to handle him physically, they would resort to "thump therapy." More than once officers had been written up. The stress levels were high for everyone.

51

One day at lunch break, one of the most experienced officers became interested in this inmate's case and the problems he had caused. He became interested after attending a seminar dealing with corrections and stress. He had taken some good tips away from the seminar and had some success in improving a relationship with his oldest son who was struggling with an addiction. Things were improving in the family as his relationship continued to get better. He got his lieutenant to allow him to be scheduled into the "maxi" unit where the infamous detainee was housed.

Shortly after obtaining the assignment, he implemented his plan. He moved from the podium to the detainee's cell and, keeping a safe distance, squared off to the small opening in the door of the inmate's room. The detainee stopped his verbal distracting to size up the "fresh meat." The officer introduced himself and asked the detainee if there was anything he could help him with. The detainee indicated, using graphic language, what help he needed. As the officer observed the detainee, he noticed that the detainee was covered with tattoos. Only his face seemed clear of them. Later, he confronted the detainee again and inquired in a non-judgmental way about the tattoos.

The detainee explained that some tattoos were related to his interest in "low riders." Low riders are cars whose frames are cut down and the cars are highly customized. They are especially popular with the Latino culture of the west coast. He also commented on the artistic quality of the tattoos and found out that the detainee was skilled at tattooing and had completed most himself. They briefly discussed some of the meanings attached to those that were visible.

Later, the officer acquired a copy of a low rider publication and after checking it out gave the copy to the detainee. As their relationship developed, the inmate's behavior improved. He began to actually swallow the medication he had been prescribed without playing games. And at the urging of the officer, he began seeing a counselor from a local university. When I last inquired, he had been returned to the general population and had been assigned to "run around" duties in his unit. Significant stress was reduced as a result of this encounter. All the interventions were done within the rules and consultation with superiors and the medical staff. This story is based on a true set of circumstances. (Some distortion is used to protect the privacy of the actual participants.)

Skills make the difference But just what is communication all about? We know that some officers can really talk with inmates and others can't. But just how are some able to handle this "talking" so effectively? Try listing what you feel may be one or two basic principles or parts of effective communication between an officer and an inmate—or even an officer and others.

List some of the things others do to make it easier for you to communicate:

_____

_____

_____

In this section, we'll be taking a close look at two fundamental communication skills and some communication principles. But first, it might be a good idea to clarify the need for these add-on skills.

53

Why it's important to communicate

Although you see and hear inmates every working day, chances are you're never sure what's really going on inside them. At the most fundamental level, officers and inmates are all human beings. But many times, it seems that the similarities stop right there. This is understandable, of course, since in the end it's obvious that inmates have different cultures and circumstances.

Understanding means effectiveness

Yet the gulf between you and any one inmate may often be frustrating. In one way you feel that you know this inmate, but in another you're sure you don't. And knowing is important. The better your understanding of any inmate, the more effective you can be in inmate management.

Communication promotes understanding

This is where communication skills become important add-ons. When you choose to use these skills, you can find out a great deal more about where individual inmates are. You can add to your understanding and action in ways that will help you defuse tension, decrease the chances of trouble, and increase your ability to handle any and all situations more effectively. The basic skills covered in Section I let you size up the situation. The add-on communication skills presented in this section let you understand the full implications of that situation and act constructively.

What are the skills?

Once you choose to communicate with inmates, you begin by putting all of the four basic skills to use: positioning, posturing, observing, and listening. As the communicative process develops, you use new skills in two important areas.

THE TWO ADD-ON SKILLS

The two communication "add-on" skills are:

1) Responding to inmates
2) Asking relevant questions

As the materials that follow make clear, responding to inmates means more than just answering a greeting—although this, too, can be important. You need to take the initiative in developing effective responses. Asking relevant questions means more than a simple *"Hey, what's going on?"* In this section you'll have an opportunity to learn the specific process to respond and ask questions. You'll also be provided with opportunities to practice both on and off the job.

Start with the basics

Position

Communicating with detainees begins by using the basic skills.

You **position** yourself at the best possible distance from the inmate—say three to four feet when you are working with a single person (although this would certainly increase if danger was imminent). This puts you close enough to see and hear everything yet not so close that you seem overly threatening. You face the inmate squarely, your left shoulder squared with his right and your right with his left. And you look directly, making frequent eye contact to let the detainee know you're really "right there." Frequent is better than intense. Three to five seconds is plenty. A stare is often threatening.

Posture

You **posture** to communicate confidence and attention. You **observe** the inmate's appearance and behavior, using visual cues to draw inferences about his feelings, relationship with you, and energy level.

Listen

You **listen** carefully, making certain to analyze all the key words and verbal indications of intensity so that you can determine just what the inmate's mood is. Only after you have mastered and put to use the basic skills will you be able to use the add-on communication skills effectively.

Like the basic skills, you take a step-by-step approach to use communication skills. First you respond to the inmate. Then you ask relevant questions. Then you respond again, this time to the inmate's answers. You will usually not just jump in and start asking questions—at least not if you're trying to get the inmate to open up and communicate with you voluntarily.

Now let's take a closer look at what the two fundamental skill areas in communicating are really all about.

Responding

THE FIRST ADD-ON SKILL   At first, responding may just sound like a fancy way of talking about the act of answering. But it really involves much more than coming up with an answer. For example, an inmate might say, *"Man, I'm really burned up about the way they've been messin' up the mail lately!"* There are several ways in which you might respond to this, even though the inmate has merely stated something and has not asked a question that would seem to need an answer. Try listing one or two types of responses you might make to this inmate.

What's important?

1) _____

2) _____

Can you think of any positive results you might get by responding in this way?

If I do...

1) _____

2) _____

Can you think of any negative things that might happen if you did not respond to the inmate's statement?

If I don't...

1) _____

2) _____

THREE LEVELS OF RESPONDING   There are three levels of responding:

1) To content
2) To feeling
3) To feeling plus meaning

57

To begin with, responding means just that—showing a clear understanding to something you have seen or heard. One of the most common complaints people have is that they are not listened to. A response should **give evidence** that you have listened. In this section, we'll take a look at several levels of responding.

Respond to content At the most basic level, you can **respond to content** by summarizing and expressing what an inmate or group of inmates has said or is doing. **Respond to feeling** At the next level, you can **respond to the feelings** shown in an inmate's words or reflected in his actions. Finally, you can **respond to both the feelings and the reasons for these feelings.** **Respond to feeling plus meaning** Each new level of responding does more to show an inmate that you are really on top of things, really seeing, hearing, and understanding.

Probably more than anything else in this manual, responding is going to seem strange to you. It's new, and you might be doubtful about its worth. There are three things to remember here.

First, this is a skill **to be added to what you already do,** rather than a skill to replace what you do. The more responses you have to choose from, the more effective you can be.

Second, by practicing the skill, you will learn the best places and ways to use it.

Third, you will grow accustomed to using the formats of responding when practicing the skill. For example, *"You are saying _____," "You feel _____," "You feel _____ because _____,"* etc. These are the guides to make it easier to succeed in the practice exercises. They will probably not seem natural to you because they don't fit your style. We understand that. Stick with them, however, until you begin to absorb the skill into your more natural delivery. Keep them if you are comfortable. They are used to enhance your skills development. Think of them as training wheels. The key is to deliver skills, not to sound cool.

Respond to content. While your use of the basic skills establishes a relationship in which inmates are more likely to cooperate and talk to you, responding is a tool you can use in the moment to communicate with inmates. Responding to content is the first step in responding to the total problem or situation. It shows an inmate that you have heard or seen what is said or done. When any person, including an inmate, knows that you are seeing and/or hearing accurately, they will tend to talk more freely. This is critical because talking gives you more of the information you need while allowing the inmate to get things off his chest.

RESPONDING at the simplest level reflects
content: *"You're saying _____."*

Use the basics   When responding to content, you are focusing on what the inmates are either saying or doing. Using what you have learned, you focus by positioning yourself for observing and/or listening to the inmates.

Respond to content   Next, you reflect on what you have seen and heard: "What are the inmates doing?" and "What is the inmate saying?" In answering both questions, stick close to what is actually going on and/or what is being said. Finally, after taking it all in and reflecting on it, you summarize what the inmates are saying or doing in your own words. You respond to the content by saying to an inmate either:

"You look (it looks) _____" or
"You're saying_____."

59

For example, *"You look pretty busy"* or *"You're saying you're pretty busy."* You respond to content when you want more information to aid you in management. This may occur when you are interrogating an inmate or when you notice unusual behavior in an inmate or group of inmates and would like to get some information from them about what they are doing. For example, you might notice a group of usually talkative inmates being very quiet. You could say to them, *"You seem pretty quiet today."* This gives them the opportunity to respond to you while also letting them know that you are **observing** them and observing them accurately. Unlike other approaches to getting information, responding to content doesn't automatically put an inmate on the defensive. It provides an opportunity for them to open up...before you need or want to question.

PRACTICE List three other examples of situations in which you might respond to content in order to get more information.

1) _____

2) _____

3) _____

Get inmates to talk instead of act The typical inmate attitude is "the inmate versus the officer." Although there is a lot of truth in this, responding can alter the "me against them" belief enough to open a line of communication with inmates. An inmate who is committed to some destructive action and who has done destructive things in the past will probably not be affected by responding to content. But such responses will give many other inmates an opportunity to talk it out rather than act it out—to share it rather than keep it inside.

Example   Here's an example: An inmate says, *"I really can't stand her. She pushes me and pushes me. Every time I see her, I want to get even."* Put aside your desire to question such an inmate (for example, *"Why do you want to do something that foolish?"*) and your desire to push her into something positive by stating a negative (*"You really want to do some more time!"*). Instead, give her a response to content: *"You're saying you really want to get back at her."* This response will encourage talk and help you get the information you need to really understand the situation before you take any action.

Instead of switching to a hostile or defensive way to counter what might be seen as an officer's usual hassling, the inmate relaxes. You're not pushing. You're not hassling. Instead, you're playing along and giving her a chance to talk it out. Also, your response gives the inmate a chance to talk about something and thereby lessen the probability that she will act. In addition, the more an inmate talks, the more you learn. And the more you learn, the easier it is to manage.

PRACTICE   Read the following examples and practice making a response to the content.

1)   While making your rounds, you come across an inmate whom you know to be pretty well behaved. Today he has stayed in his room "sick." He is sitting up in his bed. You respond...

"You look _____

_____ ."

2) An inmate says, *"I haven't received a single letter from home in over a month. I don't know what is happening. The last letter I received was such a good one."* You respond...

"You're saying _____

_____ *."*

3) An inmate says to you, *"He is going to get me this time. I know it. I haven't got a chance. I should have paid up, but I thought I could get away with it."* You respond...

"You're saying _____

_____ *."*

4) An inmate says to you, *"Sure, I know it's going down. They have it all planned out. It's going to be a real big one. Take me and shake me down so that I can give you the rest."* You respond...

"You're saying _____

_____ *."*

5) An inmate says to you, *"I'm not saying no more to you. You got all there is, which is zero!"* You respond...

"You're saying _____

_____ *."*

You may find it hard to respond to content, especially when faced with statements such as the last one. You may want to tell the inmate to watch it. You may want to explain the consequences of withholding information. But in the case from which this statement was taken, the officer did respond to content. And the inmate eventually admitted being afraid of retaliation. When this problem was discussed and resolved, the inmate gave information that led to identifying the people involved in a large contraband operation.

PRACTICE   Now write down two problems an inmate might talk to you about. Then write down what you could say in your response to that inmate's content.

1) Problem:

    _____

    _____

    Your response: " _____

    _____ ."

2) Problem:

    _____

    _____

    Your response: " _____

    _____ ."

Now repeat the exercise—but this time describe two nonverbal situations or activities involving an inmate. How would you respond to what the inmate is doing?

1) Problem:

_____

_____

Your response: " _____

_____ ."

2) Problem:

_____

_____

Your response: " _____

_____ ."

PRACTICE Practice responding to content in your work setting. Pick out situations where you want more information and respond to content. There is no doubt you will feel awkward in the beginning. Some inmates may even look at you strangely at first. Keep practicing the skill and give it an honest try. Record your own reactions and those of the inmates. Are the inmates opening up more? If you're responding well at this first level, they should be!

Respond to feeling. Every person has feelings that affect what they say and do. The nature and strength of these feelings usually determine what a person is going to do. When you respond to an inmate's feeling, you are reaching inside and encouraging the detainee to open up. The skill of responding to feelings has important implications for the management of inmates.

RESPONDING at the next level reflects
feelings: *"You feel _____."*

**Understanding
can defuse bad
feelings** Demonstrating that you understand how an inmate feels can be even more powerful than understanding the content of his actions and/or words. Showing an inmate that you understand his negative feelings can usually defuse those negative feelings. By responding to feelings at the verbal or "symbolic" behavior level, you keep the inmate's words from turning to action.

Also, responding to feelings at the verbal level can give you the necessary clues to determine a person's intention. If the detainee clams up after you have responded to the feelings, he or she is probably telling you that action is next. On the other hand, if talking continues, the detainee is indicating to you that he or she would prefer to talk it out instead of act. You all know the difference between a talking fight where the parties are looking for a way out (*"Yeah!"* versus *"Oh, yeah!"*) and a real fight where the fists will be flying any second.

Besides being able to defuse negative feelings so that words don't become actions, responding to feelings leads to greater understanding of—and by—the inmate. The inmate can't always link up feelings with the situation and is often at a loss. In addition, when you respond to positive feelings, these feelings get reinforced (unlike negative feelings). There's nothing mysterious about this. We don't enjoy our negative feelings, so we get rid of them by sharing them—by "talking it out." But we do enjoy our positive feelings. So they only become stronger when they're shared with another person.

You can begin to strengthen the positive feelings that will help an inmate act more positively simply by recognizing and responding to these feelings. As a general rule, a person who feels positive will try to do positive things while a person who feels negative will often do negative things. Thus, people tend to act in ways consistent with the way other people see them. If you put together an inmate's low self-image and the fact that others have a low image of the inmate, you can predict that the inmate will act accordingly. Positive feelings lead to positive behaviors.

Responding to content and feelings of mentally ill inmates

This may seem "out of the box" to you, but some mentally ill persons have bizarre images in their brains known as neurotransmitter disorders. Their brains don't seem to process what they see and hear normally. It is difficult to understand the content they are experiencing and difficult to reflect it. One thing you may be able to understand, however, is the **feeling** they are experiencing. You may be successful in communicating with them by letting them know this. It may be clear that they are agitated, frustrated, sad, or happy. You may never understand the content associated with the feeling, but you may be able to let them know that you are making an effort to understand and that you care about them.

PRACTICE
Can you list three situations where it would be important and useful to defuse negative feelings?

1) _____

2) _____

3) _____

Use the basics

Respond to feelings. When responding to feeling, you position and posture yourself, then observe and listen. Then you reflect for the feeling (happy, angry, sad, scared) and its intensity (high, medium, or low). Finally, you respond by saying, *"You feel _____."* (For example, *"You feel angry."*) Here the new skill involves reflecting for feeling and intensity. Adding a new skill doesn't mean discarding the old skills, of course. When reflecting for feeling, you are really asking yourself, *"Given what I see and hear, how does the detainee basically feel? Is he happy, angry, scared, or confused?"*

Intensity of feelings

High?
Medium?
Low?

After you have picked out the feeling word, you must reflect on the intensity of the feeling. For example, anger can be high in intensity (boiling mad), medium in intensity (frustrated), or low in intensity (uptight). The more accurately your feeling word reflects the intensity, the more effective your response will be. That is, your response will be more accurate and will do the job better (e.g., defuse the negative feeling). You wouldn't choose *concerned* to describe a man yelling, waving his arms, and turning red; it would be too weak. Such an understatement would probably only make him more angry. But *You feel furious* would fit fine.

PRACTICE Take each of the five basic feeling words (happy, angry, confused, sad, and scared) and write a high, medium, and low intensity word for each. For each of the fifteen feeling words you come up with, briefly describe a situation where that word might apply to an inmate.

	Happy	Angry	Sad	Scared	Confused
High	_____	_____	_____	_____	_____
Medium	_____	_____	_____	_____	_____
Low	_____	_____	_____	_____	_____

Situations where an inmate might have these feelings:

High Happy: _____

Medium Happy: _____

Low Happy: _____

High Angry: _____

Medium Angry: _____

Low Angry: _____

High Sad: _____

Medium Sad: _____

Low Sad: _____

High Scared: _____

Medium Scared: _____

Low Scared: _____

High Confused: _____

Medium Confused: _____

Low Confused: _____

PRACTICE For each of the following examples, create a response using the format *"You feel _____."* Try to match the intensity with the situation.

"I was supposed to see the nurse today, but she never showed. When I asked Officer Reynolds about it, all he said was I wasn't on the list and then he just turned away."

Your response: *"You feel* _____

_____ *."*

"I know I have to tell you but they'll find out. It'll be all over for me if they find out. They'll get me no matter where you put me."

Your response: *"You feel* _____

_____ *."*

"What can I do in here? My woman wrote and said she's got another man. She's more important to me than anything else. I've got to do something."

Your response: *"You feel* _____

_____ *."*

"I'm always being pushed around. I wouldn't care so much but I've got nobody here who is my friend. Most of them just want to turn me into a punk."

Your response: *"You feel* _____

_____ *."*

69

"This light out in the recreation area is entering my brain at night while I sleep and I think the devil is keeping track of me even when I sleep. I wake up several times at night, but I don't know how to turn it off."

Your response: *"You feel* _____

_____ *."*

"It's hard for me to believe that I'm 23 years old and I'm just learning to read and write. This school is a good thing, but all these years being a dumb jerk. Wow!"

Your response: *"You feel* _____

_____ *."*

You might practice this skill with your friends or family. When they have a problem or say something that shows their feelings, give them a *"You feel ___"* response. See if it helps them open up. Keep track of your own reactions when using your responding skill. How do you think you did (accurate or not) and why do you think so (for example, accurate because the person nodded his head and said, *"Yes, I am ___"*)?

Like any new skill, the responding skill takes practice. Be prepared to get hassled while practicing. It sounds phony until the skills blend into the natural delivery of your communication.

LEVEL 3 OF RESPONDING **Respond to feeling and meaning.** Learning how to respond to content and how to respond to feeling has prepared you to respond to feeling and meaning. Your response at this new level can put everything together; you will effectively capture the inmate's state of mind at the present.

Meaning is the reason for the feeling

By adding the meaning to the feeling, you will help yourself and the inmate understand the **reason** for his or her feelings about the situation. The reason is simply the personal meaning for the inmate about what is happening. For example, an inmate in danger of being pulled into a fight when his record is clean and his parole due might feel "scared" because "the fight could blow his chances to get out." The personal meaning of the potential fight for this inmate is that it might ruin his opportunity for parole. That is one reason **why** he is scared.

RESPONDING at the next level
reflects both **feeling** and **meaning:**
"You feel _____ because _____."

By putting together the feeling and meaning and responding to both, you show the inmate that you understand the experience being presented. This increases the chances of the inmate talking to you about the experience. In addition, for interrogation purposes, you will be able to learn more about what the inmate values and fears so that you can get a handle on the situation.

Example For example, one officer might have a hostile inmate who is uncooperative when you enter his room to shake it down:

Inmate: *"No way. You're not going to shake this cell down because some snitch told you some crap. There's nothing in here. I don't want my stuff screwed with."*

Officer: *"You feel angry because you don't want your personal items messed with."*

71

Inmate: *"That's right. I knew that damn snitch was going to run to you to get me, but I told all the guys that I'm not going to let nobody in here for no good reason."*

Officer: *"You feel tense because your reputation is on the line and you're gonna make us take you out even if it costs you."*

Inmate: *"That's right, man."* (Then he yells to other inmates) *"They ain't taking me!"*

By now the officer has the picture. This inmate has backed himself into a corner with his peers and now he can't give up. The officer wisely clears the area immediately around the inmate's room and then tells the inmate that they are going to take him out physically. Everyone can see that there won't be any unnecessary rough stuff. The responding diffused the situation and gave him an opportunity to avoid a confrontation.

Example In another situation, an inmate asks the officer a question about his work detail:

Inmate: *"Why do I have to be in the kitchen? The steam and the odors suffocate me."*

Officer: *"You feel concerned because the conditions over there make it hard for you to work."*

Inmate: *"Yeah. I get this heavy feeling in my chest and begin to wheeze after about thirty minutes. I know the kitchen supervisor thinks I'm running a game, but man, I need to get out of there!"*

Officer: *"You feel worried about your situation because you think something is wrong in your chest that is aggravated by the kitchen odors and things and you can't convince the detail supervisor that you're leveling with him."*

Inmate: *"Right. It's getting worse, too, and I don't know what to do."*

Officer: *"How about going to the infirmary in the morning to get it checked? The doctor can authorize a work detail change if he feels that your condition needs it."*

The officer understands clearly where the inmate is in the situation and where he wants (or needs) to be, and is able to suggest a possible solution. This became possible because he was able to attach an understanding of meanings to the feeling of the inmate. (**Note:** All institutional rules were applied.)

Respond to feeling plus meaning By building on what you know, you add the reason to the feeling response you have just learned. Your new way of responding becomes *"You feel _____ because _____."*

What we need to focus on is an inmate's reason (personal meaning) for the feeling. Supplying the reason means you understand why what happened is important. You do this by rephrasing (paraphrasing) the content in your own words to confirm it's importance. You are actually giving the reason for the feeling. In this way, you make the inmate's feeling clearer and more understandable. It is also important to capture whether the inmate is seeing herself as responsible or seeing someone else as responsible. Your response should reflect where the *inmate* sees the responsibility in the beginning even though

73

you may not agree. By doing this, you will have a better chance of getting him or her to open up. You can always disagree when it becomes necessary.

Consider the following situation: A detainee had been a "snitch" for a particular officer until the day he suspected that word had leaked out about it. The detainee confronted the officer, eyes narrowed and hands trembling: *"You rotten fink! You promised you wouldn't rat! Now they know about me. You really screwed me over!"*

PRACTICE Pretend you are this officer. You use your basic skills of posturing, positioning, observing, and listening to identify the basic category of the inmate's feelings: happy, sad, angry, confused, or scared.

Category of Feeling: _____

You identify the intensity of this feeling and are able to pick an accurate "feeling" word to describe the inmate's emotion:

Feeling Word: _____

Now you have to supply the reason for the inmate's feeling. What does his situation really mean to him? Who is he blaming? Why is all of this so important to him? To understand what's going on, you have to forget that you may not have leaked anything; forget that you had your reasons if you did tell someone. Forget the inmate's words and tone and language. What does this mean to him? Recognizing the meaning, you formulate a response:

Response to Feeling and Meaning: *"You feel*

_____

because _____

_____*."*

The officer who was involved knew how to initiate communication with an inmate in a tense situation like this—he recognized that failure to do so could mean trouble. He knew that the inmate's basic feeling was anger (and fear). He knew that the intensity of this feeling was high and that the inmate was really furious. And he knew that the inmate was blaming him for risking his life—the real meaning of the situation for the inmate. Knowing all of this, the officer was able to respond effectively to the inmate's feeling and what this feeling meant. *"You feel furious because you believe I put your life in danger."*

This response caught the inmate flat-footed. He had expected the officer to deny everything. Or to tell him to shut his mouth. Or to ignore the whole thing. He certainly hadn't expected the officer to respond to his situation at the same level that he, the inmate was experiencing it! Because the officer knew how to respond at this level, he was able to keep the inmate talking openly. And in a tense situation, this can mean the difference between effective management and genuine danger!

When responding to feeling and meaning, a communication interchange may sometimes go deeper than you believe you can handle. If this happens, you must consider the option of a referral. With your added understanding, your referral will be that much more specific and beneficial. But many times, your added understanding will provide you with the information you need to really manage the inmate. The payoff for you and the inmate will be rewarding. Many officers put in their time with the inmates but don't get the payoff because they lack some of the skills needed to finish off the good start that they made by being decent and fair. Responding is one way to ensure the payoff.

Practice your responding skills with inmates with whom you have been communicating. When you practice the skill, don't just give one response and say to yourself, *"Well, I did it."* Keep using your responding skills over and over again when trying to understand an inmate. When you feel he has said all he is going to say, or when you know all you need to know, then take action. But be careful about giving advice too soon. A lot of times an inmate will hold back until he sees how you react. If you tell him what to do too early, it may not be advice based on a thorough understanding of the situation. You may find that practicing these skills away from work will enable you to learn them better and will improve your communications elsewhere. Keep using these skills whenever it is appropriate and beneficial.

THE ADD-ONS

(Asking)

RESPONDING

THE BASICS
1. To content
2. To feeling
3. To feeling and meaning

76

Asking Relevant Questions

THE SECOND
ADD-ON SKILL
Everyone knows how to ask good questions, right? Well, not really—although as a correctional officer, you're probably more effective than many other people. List two steps that indicate what you do when you ask questions effectively.

**What's
important?**

1) _____

2) _____

What might happen if you failed to follow these steps in asking your questions?

If I don't...

1) _____

2) _____

What positive results might you get by making sure that you followed these steps?

If I do...

1) _____

2) _____

TWO STEPS IN
ASKING
RELEVANT
QUESTIONS

There are two basic steps involved in asking relevant questions:

1) Asking "5WH" questions
2) Reflecting on answers to questions

Having responded to an inmate accurately, you develop one or more **"5WH"** questions: who, what, where, when, why, and how. And then you **reflect** on the answer or answers given by the inmate to make sure you fully understand all the implications.

Asking questions will help you manage an inmate. If an inmate answered our questions, we would be all set. The reality, however, is that for a variety of reasons (e.g., lack of trust, his own guilt), the inmate does not answer many questions. In fact, questions will sometimes have the opposite effect—they shut off communication with inmates rather than open it up. This is because questions are often seen as the bullets of the enemy *("Cover up, here they come.")*

Use the basics plus responding

The only way questions can be effective in opening up an inmate is when they are used in **addition** to the basic skills plus responding. Using the basics plus responding can get an inmate to the point where he or she will talk openly. It is then that questions can make their contribution by obtaining some of the necessary specifics (who, what, when, where, why, and how—the 5WH system).

STEP 1 OF ASKING RELEVANT QUESTIONS

Ask 5WH questions. Answers to questions will give you the details you need. The more details you know, the better you can understand what is going on. You always want to know who is involved, what they are doing or going to do, when and where something happened or will happen, how it's going to be done or was done, and why it did or will take place.

5WH

"**Where** were you?"
"**Who** were you with?"
"**Why** were you there?"
"**What** did you actually do?"
"**When** did all this happen?"
"**How** was it handled?"

Respond, When you have information, you can take appro-
then ask priate action and/or prevent problems. Question-
asking must be used with responding during an
interrogation, interview, or when you choose to
help. Responding opens up the inmate and gives
you a chance to make sure you understand what is
being said. It also builds up trust with the inmate.
For these reasons, you should always try to
respond to an inmate's actions or words accurately
before you start asking questions. Questions then
fill in the details of the picture. Often details (reasons) come from responding skills alone. If they do
not, questions are appropriate. It's as simple as
that.

PRACTICE For each of the following situations, first make a
response and then ask an appropriate question.

You have found an inmate with lots of extra
"goodies" in her cell. You know she couldn't have
enough tickets of her own to purchase it all. When
you inquire about the "goodies," the inmate says
the following:

*"Man, can't I have some things without being
prosecuted? I used my tickets to buy these things.
I've been saving these tickets and goodies for a
long time. You just haven't looked before. A
detainee can't even take care of herself. Why don't
you find something else to do?"*

Respond: *"You feel* _____

because _____

_____ *."*

Question (5WH):   " _____

_____ ?"

"I know I'm addicted to the stuff. I tell the nurse, but she says I gotta have it, but I think it's killing me."

Respond: *"You feel* _____

because _____

_____ *."*

Question (5WH):   *"* _____

_____ *?"*

"I know it sounds weird to you, but I really hear my mother talking to me."

Respond: *"You feel* _____

because _____

_____ *."*

Question (5WH):   *"* _____

_____ *?"*

Reflect on answers to questions. It's not enough just to ask good questions. You also have to be able to make sense out of the answers (and recognize, as well, the answers you're not getting). Begin by responding to the inmate's answer (for example, *"You're saying____"* or *"So you feel____"*). Then reflect on or think carefully about an inmate's answer to your question. She may be leveling with you and giving you the information you need to manage things or even to provide assistance. She may be leveling with you as best she can, but perhaps not giving you all the information you need. Or she may be covering something up, which means that she is still not fully open.

REFLECTING means thinking about
what you have—and haven't—learned.

How does she look?

What is she doing?

What did she say?

When did it take place?

Where did it take place?

In reflecting on the inmate's answer to your question, you can reflect on the 5WH: **how** the inmate **looks** as she answers (relaxed, uncomfortable); **what** she is **doing** while she answers (facing you and making eye contact, looking away, looking down at her feet); **what** she has actually **said** (the informational content of her answer); and **what** she might have **failed to say** (any "gaps" in the way her answer fits with your question). By reflecting on these areas of concern, you can make sure that you fully understand all the implications of the inmate's answer. Once you've responded to this answer, you can ask additional questions to get the rest of the information you need.

Example

Let's imagine that you're talking with a young inmate who hasn't been inside too long. You've recognized that he's really scared stiff because of the way the other inmates have been pushing him around. And you've been able to respond to him at the level of feeling and meaning: *"So you really feel terrified because these guys just want to take you right over."* Now you're set to ask a question: *"Who are the guys who have been hassling you the most?"*

The inmate looks around quickly, then looks down at his feet. When his answer comes, it is given in a low, unclear voice: *"Oh, just some of the guys in the recreation area."*

You look at his appearance and see he's really uptight. He won't look you in the eye—he won't even speak in a clear voice. On top of this, he's answered your question with only the vaguest kind of information. In the end, his answer leaves out far more details than it includes. Upon reflection, you realize that the guy is not only scared, but is really frightened right now, in the moment, in case some of the inmates who have been after him should catch him talking to you. In other words, your reflecting lets you know that this isn't a guy who's trying to play it smart with you. He's not clamming up on purpose. Instead, he's just living in fear right there in front of you. Realizing all of this, you're able to respond even more fully and immediately to him: *"You're scared stiff right now because whoever's hassling you might get wind of us talking together."*

And the inmate looks up, surprised. He didn't know any officer could really see and hear him as he actually is. You've just grown about six inches in his eyes—maybe to the point where you suddenly seem stronger than the threat of those inmates who have been hassling him! Instead of clamming up, the young inmate keeps on talking, answering your next questions more fully. This is just what you want him to do, because in the end, you know you can gain his confidence and learn the information you need.

PRACTICE   Assume that you've been talking with an inmate about a particular situation in which he's involved. Describe the general situation below. Then write your response to what the inmate has said or done and follow it with a 5WH question. Then write out the answer that the inmate might give. After this, write out specific things that you might reflect upon. Finally, indicate what your own follow-up response might be.

Situation: _____

_____

Your Response: " _____
_____ . "

Your 5WH Question: " _____
_____ ? "

82

His Answer: " _____

_____ ."

You Reflect On: _____

_____

You Now Respond: " _____

_____ ."

Finally, practice asking questions and reflecting during your management. After you ask your question and reflect on the answer, make sure you follow with a response so that you know you're still on the right track.

Most officers ask questions. When used with the other communication skills, this skill can really bring results. Putting it all together will get you more information, increase cooperation, and maximize your management efforts.

THE ADD-ONS

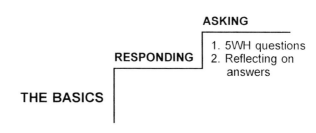

ASKING

RESPONDING | 1. 5WH questions
           | 2. Reflecting on
           | answers

THE BASICS

Now—what have you got? Jimmy was an inmate who everyone—officers and other inmates alike—invariably referred to as "a bad mother." There was a lot of respect in this phrase. You learned respect around Jimmy. How could you help it? He was 6 feet 5 inches, 275 pounds, and a former sergeant in the Green Berets. To top it off, he had a temper like a bear just coming out of hibernation who found the ground was still frozen solid.

Jimmy didn't like officers. In his time, he'd sent more than a few to the hospital. By now, the officers had figured out a drill. When they wanted Jimmy out of his cell, six of them went in and brought him out. Even then it wasn't easy. He just naturally loved to crack heads. A "bad mother" indeed!

One day a new officer who had been on the street came on to begin his duty at the jail. The old hands were happy to show him around. *"Listen,"* they said. *"You gotta meet Jimmy."*

"Jimmy?" The new guy didn't have a whole lot of experience on the job, but he knew a set-up when he saw one. *"Who's he? What's his story?"*

"You'll see... c'mon." Half a dozen seasoned officers accompanied the new man to Jimmy's cell, grinning and nudging each other. They wouldn't let the new guy get hurt or anything, but they would get a kick out of seeing his face when Jimmy tried to crush his head like a grapefruit!

"Hey, Jimmy—you got someone to see you," one of the officers told the huge inmate, unlocking the cell and moving back quickly.

Jimmy's only answer was a grunt. He had been sleeping. Now he emerged slowly from his bunk scowling and rubbing his eyes.

"What do you miserable creeps want now? Man, I'm gonna tear somebody into small pieces if you come close enough!" His eyes focused on the new guy for the first time. *"What's this, some kinda bait or somethin'?"*

The older officers expected the new guy to back off when he saw Jimmy towering over him. Instead, the new man stuck out his hand.

"I'm Ben," he said. *"I guess you're really ripped at us for just barging in on you."*

The other officers saw Jimmy's brow furrow. He'd been about to swing and they were all tensed up to jump in. But now Jimmy seemed unsure. He didn't shake. But he also didn't swing.

84

Then his face cleared. In another moment he flung his head back and laughed out loud. *"Whooeee!"* He calmed down at last and looked at the new guy. *"I knew it! I knew if I just hung around this place long enough they'd have to send in a real human being to handle me!"*

And that was it. In choosing to initiate communication instead of using force, the new officer had taken Jimmy off guard. This was a new approach. More than that, it was an indication to an inmate full of anger and hostility that maybe there still were people out there who could talk to him—even listen to him. And that knowledge made all the difference in the world to Jimmy!

What enabled the new officer to make this kind of difference, of course, were his communication skills—in particular, responding. And these are the same skills you have begun to master.

Summary of the Add-Ons

In the first section of this manual, you learned the skills you need to size up a situation. Now, working through this second section, you've learned the skills you need in order to initiate meaningful communication to improve your management— the skills involved in **responding** and **asking questions.** These skills are designed to help you manage inmates by communication. The payoffs are always for all concerned. Now it's time to move on—to go beyond sizing up and communicating and consider what's involved in controlling the situation. We'll concentrate on this topic and the skills it requires in Section III of this manual.

Section III

The Applications: Controlling Behavior

Example   **What's it all about?**

An officer whose responsibility was to control forty inmates in a unit had many assignments to delegate, many requests to answer, and many orders to give. She consistently interrupted "bull" sessions and "rap" groups to give orders. Her usual approach was to be very direct—no social amenities. A typical request was made by simply interrupting a group or an inmate's sleep by saying, *"Watson, we need to get this area policed up. Go grab a mop and get with it."* If something unusual was needed, there was never an explanation or reason, just the order. Inmates grew to resent this and complained. The officer successfully defended her behavior on the grounds that this was no "country club" and that to be courteous would be to demean her authority. She would lose the inmates' respect by being so "candy." Her philosophy was respect grows out of toughness. If inmates approached with concerns, they were normally handled in an abrasive manner. No reasons were given if requests were denied.

The officer wanted a reputation as a no-nonsense officer who does not coddle persons who couldn't make it on the street without breaking the law. The officer's parents were victims of the Depression era and had managed to get where they were the hard way and had passed along their ethics to her. If inmates completed tasks willingly or initiated helpful ideas, that was what was expected of them. The atmosphere in the unit was tense, although the "lid" was always on. She was a severe disciplinarian. Her reputation as tough was widely known. She even

87

made things tough on new officers who some-times tried to communicate with inmates or brought up new ideas that they had learned at the training center.

One evening after chow, four inmates un-bolted the motor that was used to drive the venti-lation fan on top of the unit and let it drop on the roof of the office inside the unit while this officer was filling out the log book. The motor crashed through the roof and completely severed the offi-cer's desk. Weighing 600 pounds, it was meant to crush the officer as she worked. Fortunately, she had turned away from the desk momentarily when the motor struck. The message that was commu-nicated was clear to the institution administration. Although the perpetrators were never found out, the officer's superiors had the good sense to transfer the officer to other correctional duty. It is uncertain whether the message that had been sent was received.

What went wrong? This is just one of hundreds of stories that make a similar point. Not all the ways in which officers try to control inmates are good; some are actually dangerous and more than a few have proven dis-astrous. Many ineffective methods of control have been based on the myths and folktales passed down through generations of correctional workers. The problem with the majority of these ineffective and even dangerous methods is that they treat anything other than a show of pure force as a sign of official weakness. Yet the fear of looking fearful in inmates' eyes has actually caused many offi-cers to take greater risks—like the officer in the above story. One thing is certain: as soon as an officer begins to develop effective interpersonal management skills, she begins to experience the real rewards of being able to control situations with less tension, less force—and a lot less per-sonal risk.

But let's go back to the story for a moment. What alternatives were there for this officer? Can you list a couple of important things that she might have done?

What could the officer have done?

_____

_____

For one thing, the officer could have consistently used the basic skills we covered in Section I. By using these skills—and especially those involving observation and listening—she would have had a far more complete understanding of the situation among the inmates. Even more importantly, of course, she could have responded to the inmates. This more than anything else would have let them know—in constructive rather than antagonistic terms—that she was really aware of each and every one of them. Yet even effective use of basic skills plus use of communicating skills would probably not have been enough. This officer, like every officer, needed specific yet constructive ways of **controlling inmate behavior.** This section of the manual will outline these ways—the "applications" that every officer should have.

Control is key Controlling behavior means taking charge. This is what it's all about in an institution. Without the ability to control behaviors, all the other efforts are wasted. An officer has to do everything to ensure appropriate behavior: first in the interests of the institution, then the self, and then the inmate. The same holds true for the inmate. Learning to control his own behavior is in his own interest. Control of inmate behavior leads to a secure institution. Inmate self-control leads the inmate to success. Without control, nothing productive can occur.

At the individual level, there can be great frustration among the correctional staff; officers cannot and will not work well where inmates are poorly controlled. Lack of self-control among inmates is demonstrated in murder, suicide, drugs, etc. The uncontrolled individual cannot do the constructive things that lead to success. If he doesn't die, he is doomed to come back to jail again. He is doomed to make the same mistakes over and over again. This costs him, it costs society, and it usually costs the officers who are charged with controlling the behavior of detainees who can't control their own behavior. Many mentally ill inmates have a constant problem of self-control, understanding rules, etc., not only because of their illness, but also the effects of their medication. Make certain you learn as much as possible about these factors to aid you in your management.

This section of the manual builds on previous sections. It discusses the "hows" of controlling behavior by using management skills.

What are the skills? In this final section of the manual, we'll take a close look at three different groups of skills. These skills are described as "applications" because they really represent the specific ways in which you can apply all of the other skills you've developed to manage and control behavior effectively.

THE THREE APPLICATION SKILLS There are three application skills:

1) Handling requests
2) Making requests
3) Reinforcing behavior

Unlike the skills in Sections I and II, these three groups are not necessarily cumulative. That is, you will normally be involved in handling an inmate's request or making a request of your own. In each situation, however, you will want to rein-

force the inmate's subsequent behavior—
positively if you want him to keep doing a particular thing, and negatively if you want to keep
him from doing something.

Before going further, let's examine a couple
of these skills in action.

Example   Here is a situation where an officer demonstrates
skill in management. It could be handled much
differently with more negative outcomes. It
involves both the officer making a request of an
inmate and, in turn, the inmate making a request
of the officer.

Officer: *"Lora, I'd like you to switch your work
detail with Jane for the next two weeks.
Jane has been having problems with her
neck and can't lift those buckets."*

Inmate: *"Is it okay with you if I try to get someone else to do it? I'd like to keep my
schedule as it is."*

Officer: *"I'm sorry, Lora, I know that would upset
your schedule, but I can't use anyone
else since you are the only one who can
switch on your tier. I've already checked
it out. It will only be until Jane's neck
gets better or we transfer her."*

Inmate: *"Why do you always pick on me? I'm
always the one who gets screwed on
these deals."*

Officer: *"I know this irritates the hell out of you
because it will interrupt your routine, but
it's the best I can do right now. Please
report to the work detail at 10:00 a.m.
tomorrow instead of 2:00 p.m."*

Control through skill, not force The officer in this case used his skills to control the situation. He didn't demean or put down; he didn't use sarcasm. You will observe, however, that included in his skills were firmness and reasons for his actions. There was no weakness. The inmate now knows what she is expected to do and why. The officer was even able to continue to be responsive to the inmate when she became irritated. This use of skill gets the job done and increases the probability that the inmate will feel she has been treated fairly even if she has to have her routine interrupted. This is quite a contrast when you think about how the officer from the previous example might have handled this situation.

Handling Requests

Many officers tend to think that most, if not all, inmate requests can be handled with one of two answers, both short and to the point: *"Okay"* or *"No way!"* But there's more to handling requests effectively! List one or two techniques you would use in handling an inmate's request.

What's important?

1) _____

2) _____

What would be the positive benefits of including these steps in handling inmate requests?

If I do...

1) _____

2) _____

Can you think of any negative results that might occur if you didn't include these techniques?

If I don't...

1) _____

2) _____

TWO STEPS IN HANDLING REQUESTS

In this section, we'll consider two important steps to handling requests:

1) Checking out the inmate and the situation (use the 5WH)

2) Responding to the request with a reason

The first step helps you make the best possible response. And the second step ensures that the inmate knows why you're responding, improving the chances of your request being accepted.

Before we practice the skills to handle requests, we should review the way in which institutional rules and regulations relate to the specific things to which an inmate does—and does not—have a right.

Rules, regulations, and inmate rights

Each officer and each institution is bound by certain legal and institutional requirements. Most of these things are seen to be basic rights and/or needs to which an inmate is entitled. Your institution has written regulations (not always up-to-date ones) to guide you in these areas. Following these rights and regulations usually enables an officer to establish a "decent" relationship with most of the inmates. There is always that 10 to 20 percent who react negatively no matter what you do. But by following the regulations, you can reasonably expect the inmate to do what they are supposed to do. You have taken away the excuse for negative behavior, even in the eyes of the other inmates who want to see you as the aggressor and the inmate as the victim. When you attend effectively to the inmates, you have fulfilled your basic obligations to make the institutions and the inmates more decent.

Step 1 of Handling Requests

Check out the inmate and situation. You are, and will be, bombarded by requests from inmates. Some will be legitimate, some not. You must respond to each request. Even if you ignore a request, you have responded to it and some consequence will occur that can affect your management and control. If you find this hard to believe, put yourself in a situation where you want your shift supervisor to consider one of your own requests and he ignores you. How do you feel? What message would it communicate if it happened often? What might be the consequence of it on your behavior?

CHECKING OUT REQUESTS involves
deciding if they are legitimate or not.

PRACTICE   Before you respond to any request, use your basic
skills to check out the inmate. Is he leveling with
you or is he trying to run some kind of game? You
also need to check out the situation in terms of any
rules or regulations that might apply. Using your
positioning, observing, listening, and responding
skills will be invaluable to you here. As you practice, this will become very clear to you. Now let's
look at a request situation and how you can check
things out.

Inmate Request:

*"Officer Smith, I feel sick. My stomach is upset and
I've been sweating more than usual. Can I get over
to medical?"*

What skills would be important to use in this situation?

_____

_____

What rules or regulations must be considered?

_____

_____

Another inmate makes this request five minutes
before count:

*"Officer Smith, may I run over to the recreation
area? I left my radio there and it will be ripped off if
I don't get it."*

What skills would be important to use in this situation?

_____

_____

What rules or regulations must be considered?

_____

_____

By using the sizing-up and communicating skills, you can ensure that you really know what's happening with an inmate who has a request. And by reviewing the appropriate rules and regulations, you'll have a good idea of whether the inmate's request is or is not legitimate. Remember, for the most part, the rules are not yours alone. Most are official. Don't put yourself on a limb. Now you're ready to respond to the request itself.

STEP 2 OF HANDLING REQUESTS **Respond with a reason for your decision.** The new skill involves choosing the action you're going to take—your decision—and giving the inmate your reason. Remember, giving the inmate a reason is **not** a sign of weakness. On the contrary, it is the best way to minimize future gripes. If you turn the inmate down, he won't be able to complain that you didn't tell him why. And if you grant his request, he'll know that it was just for this one situation for a good and clear reason.

RESPONDING with a reason eliminates hassles.

Reason for action An officer has three avenues of action to an inmate's request. In each case, he should give some reason for his action unless he is positive the inmate already knows the reason. Here are the simplest forms these responses can take:

"Yes" *"Yes I'll do (it) _____ because _____."*

"No" *"No I won't do (it) _____ because _____."*

"I'll check" *"I'll look into (it) _____ because _____."*

How you decide   In each instance, the officer bases his or her reasoning on the laws and regulations of the institution. In cases where inmates need or request something beyond what they are entitled to by law and regulation, each inmate's behavior (past and present), what is asked for, the way it is asked for, and the information you have gained by checking things out should determine your response. For example, an inmate might ask you, *"Hey man, how about a phone call?"* You answer, *"No, I can't allow you to have a call; you have had your quota today and extra calls are only possible through the counselor (or case manager)."* In doubt, ALWAYS run it by your supervisor!

Take care of   While there may be an option in the case above,
basic needs   some things—like a man's food—cannot be withheld. You may have other options for an abusive inmate who demands his meal (e.g., write him up) but you can't deny him food. Knowing the law and the regulations of your institution will definitely make your job easier—if you turn someone down because of the rules, then it's the institution's rule, not yours. By taking care of the basic needs of the inmate, these headaches and other security problems (tensions) will be greatly reduced.

Taking care of basic needs is a "must" in any relationship. It would be very hard for an inmate to believe you wanted to communicate and assist him if you did not attend to his basic needs—that is, if you did not give him what he was entitled to. Dealing with such needs is a concrete way to build trust, which will make it likely that the inmate will be more cooperative.

PRACTICE In the following examples, decide if you would communicate or assist or not, and write down the reasons why.

Frank is an inmate who has served five years. When he first came in, he was a hard case— always causing trouble, late for work detail, etc. About two years ago, he finally got the message. Since that time, he has behaved really well with the officers, but not always so decently with the other inmates. Frank has never become violent, but he has been abusive with other inmates. With you, he has always been polite and cooperative. Today he comes to you, tells you he is sick, and wants to "lay in." Respond with a reason.

_____

_____

_____

_____

Joanne is a good inmate, but lately she has become very depressed because her husband has left her. She doesn't help you as much as she did, but she still doesn't get in your way. She wants to make an extra call to check up on her children. Respond with a reason.

_____

_____

_____

_____

Now examine the following inmate requests. Determine if they are legitimate or not and then respond using the following formats:

Legitimate: *"Yes, I'll do (it)*   _____

because   _____

_____*."*

Not Legitimate: *"Yes, I'll do (it)*   _____

because   _____

_____*."*

Not Sure if Legitimate: *"I'll look into (it)*

because   _____

_____*."*

Think of *legitimate* as meaning the inmate either deserves it by law, regulation, or his behavior. After the "because" in your response, tell him why you are doing what you say.

"My laundry is messed up. Will you let me wear this 'free world' shirt?"

Your answer: _____

_____

Reason: _____

_____

"When the hell are you going to check my account? I told you it was screwed up, huh?"

Your answer: _____

_____

Reason: _____

_____

"Excuse me, Officer, I need to run up and see the chaplain. Can I have a pass?"

Your answer: _____

_____

Reason: _____

_____

PRACTICE Now list five requests that would be considered legitimate at your institution and five requests that would not be legitimate. For the latter, indicate why. For example, in some institutions, inmates in a certain unit are entitled to decorate their cells while others are not. Thus an officer might say to an inmate who is below the authorized level, *"No you cannot because you have not yet earned that privilege."* Be as specific as possible.

List five legitimate requests inmates could make:

Legitimate Requests

1) _____
2) _____
3) _____
4) _____
5) _____

Now list five non-legitimate requests and the reasons why they are not legitimate.

Non-Legitimate Requests

Request	Why
1) _____	_____
2) _____	_____
3) _____	_____
4) _____	_____
5) _____	_____

PRACTICE Finally, to sharpen your skills, keep a list of requests made of you and decide if each is legitimate.

When you return to work, listen to the requests of inmates. Decide if you should help them with the request or not. Formulate a response that lets them know what you are going to do and why.

CONTROLLING BEHAVIOR

(Reinforcing)

(Making Requests)

HANDLING REQUESTS

THE ADD-ONS   1. Checking things out

THE BASICS   2. Responding with reason

Making Requests

The same officers who answer every request with a flat "yes" or "no" may also be in the habit of making every request in the form of a direct order. While such orders are necessary at times, they are not the whole story. Making requests effectively involves a couple of different steps. List two important steps below:

What's important?

1) _____

2) _____

What would you gain by taking these steps when you needed to make a request?

If I do...

1) _____

2) _____

What would you possibly lose if you didn't take these steps?

If I don't...

1) _____

2) _____

Two Steps in Making Requests

The two steps in making requests are:

1) Checking things out (using the 5WH)
2) Taking appropriate action

As before, you check things out to ensure that you don't make the wrong move—a move that might increase tension. Once you've done this, you can decide whether the best action will involve a simple request, an order, or even direct physical action.

Check things out. Since the procedures here will be the same as those involved in handling inmate requests, there's no need to go back over them. Your aim should be to understand the situation involving the inmate you plan to have do something. Is he with his friends? If so, what's his relationship to them? Will he believe he's losing face if you give him an order and therefore react antagonistically? By using your basic sizing-up skills and your responding skills, you can make sure that whatever action you take, your request will be effective.

Using basic skills

Know the situation

CHECKING THINGS OUT involves the use of your basic and responding skills.

Take action. Making requests of inmates is routine in corrections. Many requests are made each shift and often little thought is given to the impact of requests on the control of inmates. Yet as many of you know, it's how the request is made that makes the difference, not necessarily the content of the request. Test this logic on your own situation.

TAKING ACTION means selecting the best way to make your request.

How you ask may mean more than what you ask!

To get an inmate to do something, remember to be specific. You should identify what you want done and when. Telling an inmate in this manner keeps you clean. You've put it right out there for him and anybody else to see. Many officers have found that a polite request is most effective in getting an inmate to do what he is told. Of course, there are officers who feel that the inmates don't deserve politeness or that it makes an officer look weak. But you were brought up with good manners, and the question is, are you going to let an inmate bring you down to his level?

In addition, when an inmate doesn't do something reasonable when asked reasonably, then it is he who looks weak. Moreover, by being initially polite, you've given the inmate the opportunity to go the easy way. Now it's his responsibility if you have to go the hard way.

Mild or polite format Some of you are going to find it difficult to use a polite format, but many officers have found that it is more effective. It gets the results you want. A mild (polite) request can take the form *"Would you (please) _____,"* or it can take the form *"I would appreciate it if you would _____."*

Direct format When you make an inmate request, the most direct method is simply to identify what you want and then use the format *"I want you to _____."* But because inmates will frequently resent authority, if you are telling them to do something, you may have fewer hassles if you use a soft request format.

Softening a request Examples are *"I'd like you to do _____,"* or *"Would you stop _____."* You can soften the statement even more by using polite words. For example, *"I'd like you to please stop _____."*

Get stronger when necessary What format you use for making a request will depend on the situation and the particular inmate. If an inmate abuses the milder method, you are always free to move to a stronger position, including a direct order. As indicated above, the point is to get the job done—to have the inmate do what you want. Experienced officers agree that it is generally easier if direct confrontations can be avoided.

PRACTICE Now practice achieving control by telling an inmate your request and what you want him to do. Let's take the inmate who is hung up on respect. In front of a group of inmates, he spits in your direction as you walk by. Your aim is to get him to show more respect to you as an officer and to obey sanitation rules. Write below what you would say and do to make an appropriate request.

What you would do: _____

_____

What you would say: " _____

_____ ."

Use responding skills You may also want to use your responding skills in taking action. For example, you encounter an inmate who is where he should not be. You position yourself so that you can see him, but he cannot see you. You observe for a while because he appears to be doing nothing else wrong. Then you move into position so that he can also see you. You approach cautiously. As you approach, you recognize the inmate as a new man. He makes no sudden moves. In fact, he greets you: *"Hello, Officer."* You give him the benefit of the doubt in the sense that you are open to what he is going to say. The inmate is a new inmate and you haven't seen or heard anything to make you intensify your security efforts. Using your basics:

You: *"Hi _____. You seem to have drifted off from the rest of the group."*

Inmate: *"I guess so. I just wanted to get off by myself for a while."*

You: *"I see. I guess you can get a feeling of being closed in sometimes being in here, but you can't drift off to this area because it is unauthorized."*

105

Inmate: *"I didn't realize that."*

You: *"Yeah, I'd like you to move back away from here and nearer that group."*

PRACTICE   There may be times when you want to start with a direct order to take immediate action. List two examples when you would give a direct order or take immediate action without making a request. Give the reason why you would do this.

Direct Order First:

Situation 1: _____

_____

Why: _____

_____

Situation 2: _____

_____

Why: _____

_____

Immediate Action First:

Situation 1: _____

_____

Why: _____

_____

Situation 2: _____

_____

Why: _____

_____

CONTROLLING
BEHAVIOR

(Reinforcing)

MAKING
REQUESTS

HANDLING   1. Checking things out
REQUESTS   2. Taking action

THE ADD-ONS

THE BASICS

Reinforcing Behavior

THE THIRD
APPLICATION
SKILL The reason people do anything is because of the experience or perception of consequences (positive or negative). Behaviors change when there are consequences. Inmates have (as strange as it may seem) been rewarded for deviant behavior. It is often tied to a culture. Some of the most negative behavior is reinforced. People get social approval from gang members; a feeling of ecstasy from dope; a sense of power from getting revenge, etc. A lot of positive feeling is temporary, so the action must be repeated as soon as possible. Substance abuse is clearly an example. Letting a detainee off easy is not really in his or her best interest unless we can guarantee that positive change occurred, and of course we cannot.

In addition to the rewards for negative behavior, many inmates live in a world where being straight and decent is seen as negative and weak. They didn't (haven't) experienced sufficient reward for new behaviors because for the most part, these opportunities aren't available in most institutions. To turn this crazy picture around, institutions and officers must be sure to reward or punish the appropriate behaviors. Also, the punishments and rewards themselves have to be appropriate. The inmate has to experience an action as a reward or a punishment. The reward must also be seen as worth the price and the punishment of the deed in order to be effective in changing behavior. If you send a detainee to isolation as punishment, and he ends up with a private cell and no loss of privileges, you may not really be punishing. In fact, you may actually be rewarding a negative behavior. You may be rewarding yourself by getting rid of the detainee for a while to bring you some peace.

The way this reinforcing process works is interesting sometimes. You restrict someone's behavior to hopefully change behavior and you are the beneficiary. I often have to remind the skeptics that although this training has the illusion of teaching how to treat the detainee nicely, it's clear that the big payoff is for the officers and the institution—less stress, less danger, etc. The inmate is always testing to find out what the limits are and who is really in control. Many inmates want to know "how much do I have to screw up before somebody tells me to stop?" Once an inmate knows who is in control, he will reduce his testing behavior. Having skills results in the inmate being in your control instead of your being in the inmate's control.

Hopefully, *negative reinforcement* and *punishment* being similar in meaning will not confuse you. There are theoretical differences. An example would be to remove an inmate from an activity being enjoyed (as a negative reinforcement). Does placing the detainee in isolation serve as a punishment or a part of reinforcement? Psychologists can explain many accurate nuances to the science of reinforcement behavior. To defend the way we use it in this manual, I call it "jailhouse reinforcement theory." "Reinforcement theory" is very theoretical. There are many theories. In this manual, positive reinforcement is generally approval. Negative reinforcement is disapproval. Punishment generally means a severe restriction: loss of freedom, etc.

Using the space below, try listing one or two ways in which you might use reinforcement to get an inmate to stop doing something he should not be doing—and then hopefully to keep him from doing it again.

What rewards can you use?

What's important?

1) _____

2) _____

What do you think would happen as a result of your providing this kind of reinforcement?

If I do...

1) _____

2) _____

What might happen if you did not supply any reinforcement?

If I don't...

1) _____

2) _____

TWO WAYS TO REINFORCE
There are two kinds of reinforcement: **verbal** and **nonverbal**. Rather than review these in separate sections, we will consider them together.

VERBAL AND NONVERBAL REINFORCE-MENT

Warning
You have several options for giving verbal reinforcement. If a warning is appropriate, you can use a format such as *"If you do not do _____ then (negative) _____ will happen."* The first blank would be the behavior you want to have the inmate start or stop, and the second blank would be the consequences. If a warning is not appropriate, the format would be *"Since you have _____ (behavior), then _____ (consequences)."*

Approval
Another kind of reinforcement is personally expressing your approval of the inmate's behavior. The format here would be *"That's a really helpful thing"* or *"Stella, this place is looking good."*

110

REINFORCING means using **verbal** and
nonverbal rewards and punishments.

Force is risky!   Nonverbal reinforcement (physical force) should
only be used where there is a threat of physical
harm to you, to the inmate, or to other inmates.
The risk of such reinforcement is high and it
should be used as a last alternative. Not to be
confused with moving a stubborn detainee...you
can reward the stubbornness. The most common
and some say the most effective reinforcing are
nonverbal gestures and facial expressions that we
use so frequently, we often do not think of them
as reinforcers: the smiles, nods, and head movement. You can examine these in more detail later
in some of the exercises.

Example   There was one officer who was told by a snitch
that an inmate had a shank in his cell. The officer
went to the cell and called the inmate out so that
he could shake down the cell. The inmate
appeared reluctant, so the officer grabbed him
and pulled him out. The inmate had the knife hid-
den in his shirt and shanked the officer. The officer should have thought through the situation
before attempting to get the inmate out of his cell.
Instead, he got caught up in his need to reinforce
the inmate with physical force and to appear
tough.

Reinforcements are not threats. As you know,
you never threaten what you won't and/or can't
do, and you never give consequences on which
you don't intend to follow through. When you
reinforce negatively, you are not setting up a
challenge; you are only making clear where it's at
and what **will** happen (what the inmate is going to
force you to do or what you are required to do).
You can't reinforce if you are out of control. When
you are out of control, you can only threaten. And
this may put the inmate in control. Your manner

111

and tone of voice should be firm but calm. For example, you might say *"I'm giving you a direct order to stop. If you do not, then I'm going to have to write you up."*

Negative reinforcements

List all the punishments you can use and the behavior you might give them (e.g., write up for refusing to obey a direct order). This exercise is not asking you to repeat things from any book you have that lists violations and punishments, although you ought to know the contents of such a book, if it exists.

List possible punishments (severely restricts freedom).

Punishments:

1) _____
2) _____
3) _____
4) _____
5) _____

List behaviors that you might punish.

Behaviors:

1) _____
2) _____
3) _____
4) _____
5) _____

It's just as important to positively reinforce or reward good behavior as it is to negatively reinforce or punish poor behavior. In fact, trouble can sometimes get started simply because an officer doesn't know how to keep things going as well as they have been going! The effective officer knows when inmates are handling things well and does everything possible to keep them on track. In addition, he positively reinforces even occasional good work by detainees who may mess up at other times. This officer may tell the detainee who always works well, *"Glad to see you're doing your usual fine job, Ben—I know I can always count on you."* This sort of verbal reinforcement helps the man keep going in a constructive direction.

The officer may also call *"Way to go, Bill!"* to an inmate who has just done his first positive thing of the day. The officer knows it's important for this inmate to recognize when he's on track— just as he has to realize when he's off track.

PRACTICE

Positive reinforcements

List all the positive reinforcements you can think of and the inmates' behavior for which you would give positive reinforcement (e.g., compliment and/or high rating for always being on time).

Rewards:

1) _____

2) _____

3) _____

4) _____

5) _____

Now list the behaviors you might want to reward.

Behaviors:

1) _____

2) _____

3) _____

4) _____

5) _____

PRACTICE Let's practice a few negative and positive reinforcements.

An inmate has been harassing a group of inmates working on a special detail. After asking him to stop, he reduces his harassment, but not completely:

Your reinforcer: _____

_____

An inmate has, on several occasions, been a few seconds late for meetings, each time a little bit later.

Your reinforcer: _____

_____

An inmate whose living area has been dirty has been warned in the past; you notice during inspection that it is now spotless.

Your reinforcer: _____

_____

An inmate has exhibited withdrawal and depression. You now notice him voluntarily taking part in a cell-house clean-up.

Your reinforcer: _____

_____

PRACTICE Now practice giving reinforcements to the inmates. What are the results of adding reinforcements to your other application skills? Again, reinforcements are not **threats**. They should flow naturally from you because of concrete behaviors of the inmates. Ask yourself, *"Should this behavior be rewarded, punished, or ignored?"* Whenever you reward or punish, identify the behavior involved and the reason.

114

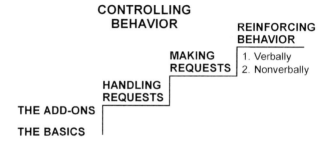

CONTROLLING
BEHAVIOR

REINFORCING
BEHAVIOR

MAKING
REQUESTS

1. Verbally
2. Nonverbally

HANDLING
REQUESTS

THE ADD-ONS

THE BASICS

Controlling behavior uses all of your skills. This means having the most effective security in your area without having to meet each distraction with force. Your intelligence and experience combined with your new skills will enable you to manage things in a constructive way. Inmates and fellow officers will be affected by your leadership. They will be able to carry out the routines of living and interacting together in reasonable ways. The inmate will be in your hands. You will be able to communicate to reduce tension, hassles, frustrations, and problems, and other officers will model your behavior because it is effective in achieving results with minimal distractions.

Remember, security is your primary concern. As an officer, your duties each day require you to manage all inmates. Managing inmates with effective skills will increase the chances that your job will be easier. Sure, there are many inmates who will only respond to a hard-line approach and a show of strength. But there are others who can and will learn to cooperate. And for every one of these inmates you are able to reach with your new skills, there's one less security problem for your institution.

Now—what do you have? Let's really see how you've progressed.

You come on duty in the rec area. Your supervisor is there and she approaches you. She asks you to check out a group of detainees near the fence. What are the first things you do? Outline each step you would take to implement the request.

Step 1: _____
Reason: _____

Step 2: _____
Reason: _____

Step 3: _____
Reason: _____

Step 4: _____
Reason: _____

Step 5: _____
Reason: _____

Move toward the group until you are at the best distance—close enough to see their faces clearly, yet staying in the perimeter so that you can still see everyone in the yard and stay safe. You can listen as you're moving in just in case you can pick up any key words or expressions before inmates clam up.

You should observe everything possible about the inmates: individual and collective appearance, behavior, and environment. This will give you a good idea as to what's going on.

You draw any inferences you can about the inmates' apparent feelings, their relationships with one another and with you, their levels of energy, and the things on which they might focus their attention.

You should make an initial judgment as to whether this is a "trouble" or a "no trouble" situation. If you have really been polishing your basic skills, you can accomplish this on a tentative basis before you ever open your mouth.

All right. Let's say the inmates stop talking as you come close. They all watch you except one smaller inmate sitting behind the group in question. From what you can see of him, he's looking down at the ground. The front inmates are holding their bodies tensely, and the inmate in back seems slumped and dejected. The front men look nervous. The clues to this are the way they dart little glances at one another. You decide there could be trouble. Recognizing one of the men in front, you speak to him:

"Hello, Lewis. What's happening here?"

"We're not doing anything. We're just minding our own business."

PRACTICE Okay. Outline with as much detail as possible the next two steps you would take.

_____

_____

_____

_____

That's right. You'd begin by responding to Lewis's reluctance to talk. Once you did this, you would request that he and the other men move aside so that you could see the man in back. He comes forward at your request, his eyes still on the ground. He looks scared to death. Lewis, apparently the ringleader among the other inmates, looks nervous and defiant at the same time. What do you do now?

_____

_____

_____

_____

One action would be to request that all the inmates except for Lewis separate and move away from the area. Next you should respond again to Lewis's reluctance and then ask in a direct and firm manner that he explain to you what's been happening.

Why not question the inmate who looked scared? Chances are that wouldn't be a wise move. The other inmates appear to have been intimidating him. If they think you've gotten him to talk, they may just give him a worse time later. But if you can get Lewis to open up, you can really get to the bottom of things.

Let's assume you continue to use your communicating skills with Lewis. You question him, respond to his answers as fully as possible, then question him some more. Finally he opens up with you. He admits that he and the others were trying to shake down the other man. The way he lays it out, it wasn't any big thing—just some strong guys leaning on a weaker guy because they were bored and didn't have anything else to do. Now—what do **you** do?

_____

_____

_____

_____

If you indicated that your best move would be to assign Lewis and his friends some extra work as a negative reinforcement—or restrict his privileges for a brief time—you're right. The best way to overcome a negative or destructive tendency of this kind is to show the inmate that it only gets him messed up. Had it turned out that Lewis was involved in something constructive, of course, you would have done just the opposite—provided some positive reinforcement for his actions.

One more thing—and an important one! Once Lewis starts functioning more constructively—in fact, the first time he does **anything** right—you should go out of your way to positively reinforce him. Only in this way can you counter the hostility that negative reinforcement may promote and keep someone like Lewis moving in a positive direction.

Perhaps all of this sounds simple. Yet how many officers do you know who would simply charge over to the group and yell _"All right you guys, break it up!"_ And in doing so, increase hostility, and learn little or nothing in the process. A missed opportunity!

If you found you did well in this final exercise, you've got a right to be proud of yourself. It might be well to take a final moment to consider just why this pride is justified—and important.

We've talked a lot about security and management in this manual. These are obviously the most important aspects of your work. Yet some of you may have wondered why we haven't brought up the familiar matter of inmate rehabilitation. We chose to pass on this topic for a very simple reason: there's no point in making promises you can't keep. And at this point it would be foolish to promise any officer that he could learn all that is needed to completely rehabilitate even one inmate, never mind an entire population.

But we can make one promise: the skills you have learned in this manual are the **first step** toward meaningful rehabilitation of inmates. This means that you have done more than master specific methods of managing inmate populations. It means that you have more reasons than you may have suspected to be proud.

You've developed professional skills to do a professional's job. You've helped lay to rest that familiar stereotype that "civilians" have of the correctional officer as a brutal, brainless machine that delights in keeping people locked up. And you've gone beyond. You've begun to act upon one of the most basic equations in all of human history.

HUMAN ACTIONS DETERMINE HUMAN REACTIONS

The cornerstone of the interpersonal management skills you've learned is decency—simple human decency. You've got a job to do. But in doing it, you've learned how you can handle inmates like the human beings they are. And in return, you'll be able to promote more decent and constructive behavior on their part. This process involves what has been called "the principle of reciprocal behavior"—a fancy way of saying that we all get back what we give. In your case, you've learned how to invest your work with professional effectiveness—with real skills—and still give inmates the decent treatment they need to develop more constructive patterns of behavior.

Yes, you've got a great deal of which to be proud. Let the committees in Washington draw up endless reports making recommendations about rehabilitation. Let the bleeding hearts write innumerable letters about brutality to their favorite newspaper editors. Let the rest of the world view the prime-time television image of correctional institutions as the garbage can of society. Let all that go.

As long as you've got the skills to communicate with inmates, you'll be able to reduce tension and get inmates to open up with you.

As long as you've got the skills to control inmates, you can manage their behavior in increasingly constructive ways.

And as long as you can put all of these skills together, inmates realize they're being treated decently. You're doing more than all the committees and letter-writers and TV viewers in the world to rehabilitate the people who are your charges.

Yes, you've got a right to your pride now, because you are bringing both professional skills and simple decency to one of the toughest jobs in the world.

About the Author

Dr. Steve Sampson is the founder and president of SoTelligence®, Inc., which offers a series of courses, seminars, workshops, and intensives designed to teach people social and emotional intelligence and provide them with the skills necessary to develop, grow, and maintain healthy and rewarding personal relationships—at work, at home, and in their community.

Today, most training programs focus on teaching concepts that are of limited value when the participant leaves the classroom. Like many self-help books, these programs cover a lot, but they don't provide the attendee with the necessary "how to" instructions to accomplish the goals of the course.

At SoTelligence®, we employ a Tell-Show-Do-Feedback method of training where participants can learn about a concept, see it demonstrated by certified trainers, practice it in a safe and supportive environment, and receive (as well as give) feedback to others during practice rounds. This method has been shown to provide the best opportunity for participants to *develop new skills* and actually *change their behaviors*. For more information, contact us at www.SoTelligence.com.